"Steve Pipe has made a marvellous contribution: finding out and reporting in clear terms what really works. This book is invaluable."

David Maister

Author of *Managing the Professional Service Firm* and *The Trusted Advisor*

"Breathtakingly refreshing. This book shows that Accountants can (and actually do) do great things. Read this and be inspired and proud of what members of the profession do when they put their minds to it."

Paul Dunn

Chairman of B1G1 and author of *The firm of the future*

"This is the most exciting book I have read in the last two years. It should be required reading for every public accountant, and I can't wait to share it with my CPA clients in the USA because 99 percent of it applies anywhere in the world. Exceptionally useful, insightful and practical."

Dave Cottle CPA

Author of *Clients4Life*

"This is the most practical and personally beneficial business book I have ever read. It's packed with insights, useful tips and systems from the most forward looking accountancy firms that any practice can use, from sole practitioner to large partnerships. It is so inspiring and motivational to hear how they actually do it and the ways they apply Steve Pipe's golden rule of proactivity. It has given me so many different ideas and initiatives that I can start putting in place right away. I highly recommend it to every accountant who is serious about building a great practice."

Andrew Rhodes FCA CTA

Managing Partner of Sobell Rhodes, Accountancy Age Medium Size Firm of The Year

"Steve Pipe has written an inspiring book! The firms profiled in The UK's Best Accountancy Practices are proof that the traditional business model based upon "We sell time" is dying. It is possible for the profession to innovate new business models based upon being Professional Knowledge Firms, with an understanding that "We sell Intellectual Capital." Focusing on creating and capturing value is the only path for the profession to stay relevant.

Read – and learn from – the stories of the firms that are blazing the trail others will inevitably follow. It's the difference between remaining a Firm of the Past, or, like a chrysalis, emerging as a Firm of the Future. The choice is yours."

Ronald J. Baker

Founder of The VeraSage Institute (www.verasage.com) and author of *The Firm of the Future* and *Implementing Value Pricing: A Radical Business Model for Professional Firms*

"A book about people who said 'I can'. Read it and be inspired. And, wherever you are in the world, get out your highlighter pen since there are great ideas that have been proven to work on every page."

John Haylock

Author of *Absolute Certainty: How to give your clients exactly what they want –* www.absolute-certainty.com

"Hearing about what real people have actually put into practice is far more convincing than an encyclopaedia of theorising. It is therefore far more likely to inspire others to take action. A great job."

Nigel Bennett FCA

Managing Partner of Accountancy Age Medium Size Firm of The Year, Hallidays

"Steve Pipe has done a superb job of analysing the heartbeat of the best performing firms in the UK. There are hundreds of ideas which will keep an enterprising firm busy for many years. The level of detail is extraordinary. Learn from this research and profit in a major way".

Rob Nixon

Australasian consultant and author of *Accounting Practices Don't Add Up – why they don't and what to do about it!*

"Insightful and challenging. Definitely the book to take to the desert island – then you would want to come back excited at the prospect of implementing innovative strategies that will revolutionise your business."

Mark Lloydbottom FCA

Consultant and author of *Defining Edge Practice Management Strategies*

"I have read this book with much sadness and regret. Why? Simply because as I reflect on my 30 years in practice as a Chartered Accountant I realise how little we really added value for the client and, as a result, how much more me and my partners could have added value to our own bank accounts. I practised in a time (1970-2000) when the professional accountant was simply a bean counter, a historian who simply reacted to client's needs when it suited him of course. "I'm a professional not a business person; they'll get it when it suits me". Oh dear, oh dear I reminisce.

With Steve's AVN he has revolutionised the profession for the sake of both parties, the client and the advisor and I only wish I was starting out now. There are literally hundreds of gem ideas in the book and if any young accountant is setting up now he/she should buy this book and devour every word. It will become a classic text book for the modern day professional."

Will Kintish FCA
Founder and chief presenter at Kintish Networking Skills - www.kintish.co.uk

"Steve Pipe has produced irrefutable evidence that supports what I've been telling anyone who'd care to listen for years... 'The Accounting Profession is SEXY!' Yes, I said that out loud, didn't I?

But let's face it, what other profession can present practitioners with regular opportunities to help clients raise finance, make more money, create new jobs, build new factories and generate new wealth?

Picking the right clients to work with, presenting the right types of services (that add value to your clients' businesses) and billing based on value rather than time is the way forward for our profession. Steve Pipe hits the nail bang on the head with this publication.

He describes step-by-step how to break away from the pack and use the knowledge we gain over our careers to our own benefit. Those who think that time is money must have very strange clocks. This book proves that KNOWLEDGE = MONEY, if you know how to position this with clients. Pipe shows you how it's done – not from theory that just might work in practice, but from real examples that HAVE worked and DO WORK.

It's about time the accounting profession stopped making excuses for itself and realized the tremendous value it can add to its clients, and unashamedly start charging appropriately. This book is the roadmap for how to do it.

If you want to make your accounting firm more successful, then there's only one thing to do: Buy this book, read it, devour it, adapt its ideas to your own firm, and reap the rewards you shall so dearly deserve!"

Steve McIntyre-Smith
Author, speaker and consultant to the public accounting profession

"Back in 1998 Steve changed my life with his advice on how to transform my practice. And now this book proves once again that he is the UK's leading thinker in the accountancy profession. It contains dozens of profoundly powerful insights and proven ideas to improve any practice, and is compulsory reading for every practising accountant who cares about their clients and their future."

Mark Wickersham FCA

Author of *Effective pricing for accountants*

"This shows the way Accountancy Practices should be run as a business and Steve has captured this brilliantly. A truly inspiring book."

Rob Walsh FCA

Founder and Managing Director of award winning accountants Clear Vision

"Not all accountants are frustrated lion-tamers, they are mostly ordinary men and women. However, by understanding that profit is merely a product of consistent, value-based behaviours, ordinary accountants can create extraordinary businesses. Placing clients, and the people that look after them, at the absolute centre of those behaviours, ensures success. Steve Pipe's remarkable book doesn't preach or theorise, it invites you to look in the mirror, it lets you see, simply and digestibly, how to do it."

Robert Brown FCA

Managing Director of Landers, Accountancy Age Small Firm of The Year

"When picking up this book, I felt like I was a child going into a sweet shop and being told I can help myself from anything that's on display. This book is really as good as that. It takes one's breath away in the way it presents an extraordinarily wide range of really attractive options to help one grow one's practice."

Hugh Williams FCA

Founder of award winning accountants H M Williams & Co and author of *Life without timesheets*

"Steve has done something great for the profession by clearly proving how accountants can be remarkable and achieve remarkable results. Any accountant wanting to improve their firm's performance and their quality of life MUST read this book and make these insights their own."

Paul Shrimpling

Founder of Remarkable Practice Ltd and author of *Bamboo Marketing*

"Brilliant. This book is an invaluable reference resource for managing partners, or anyone analysing their firm's performance.

Interestingly, most of the ideas common to the successful firms arise from the realisation that accountancy is a language. It's a language that can summarise a large number of transactions, some complex, and communicate useful information to a business owner or manager to help them make business decisions.

It's clear that some accountants have found ways of using this language, and developing tools, that clients find useful and valuable. Steve Pipe has done the profession a great service by collating these ideas.

Perhaps accountancy can regain its proper reputation as a management tool rather than just as a scorecard!"

Mark Spofforth FCA

President of the Institute of Chartered Accountants in England and Wales (2012-2013) and partner at Spofforths

The UK's best accountancy practices

Steve Pipe

A catalogue for this book is available from the British Library

ISBN 978-0-9551007-2-7

First published 2011 by:

>   Added Value Solutions Limited
>   7 Midland Way
>   Barlborough
>   Derbyshire
>   S43 4XA

This edition published in 2011

Edited by Caroline Swain

Designed and set by Barbara Linton

Printed in the United Kingdom by:

>   The MPG Books Group
>   Bodmin and King's Lynn

This book is dedicated to the
extraordinary accountants
featured within these pages
and to the many others I have
learned from over the years.

Contents

Excellence in the accountancy profession

This book is about excellence in the accountancy profession.

My fervent hope is that the many Examples of Excellence it contains, will not only inspire the rest of the accountancy profession to want to get better, but will also provide the proven and practical insights that make "getting better" easier.

There is no theory in these pages. Just example after example of what real UK accountancy practices have done in the last few years, and are still doing today, to generate better results for their clients, their communities and themselves.

Some of the Examples of Excellence are 'whole firm' case studies. Others focus on a single system or process. But in every case, the firms in question are shining examples of what is possible and how to make it happen.

None of them would claim to be the best at everything. In fact, many of them are too modest to tell you they are the best at anything. But, as you will see, they are all superbly good at one or more thing.

Of course, their clients know that already. Which is no doubt why, on average, the firms featured in this book have received nine times as many recommendations on LinkedIn as firms not featured here.

The message is therefore crystal clear.

If you are an accountant, make your firm more like the Examples of Excellence within these pages.

And if you are a business owner, insist that your accountants become more like these Examples of Excellence.

Extraordinary candour, remarkable detail

The firms featured have been extraordinarily candid, open and detailed in their descriptions of what makes them so successful. For example, some of the Examples of Excellence reveal in precise detail how they have:

1

- Saved clients an extra £7.6 million in tax

- Doubled their turnover in 18 months

- Not only survived the sudden loss of one of two partners, but actually thrived in the face of it

- Quadrupled profits since 2009

- Generated £176,000 in extra fees from a new service line, despite initial scepticism and resistance from partners

- Helped a client generate enough cash to rescue an ailing business and save over a hundred local jobs

- Earned annual profits in excess of £250,000 per partner

- Won countless business awards

- Transformed their life-work balance so that they work standard office hours, don't work on Friday afternoons or weekends, and take 10 weeks holiday a year

- Eliminated debtors

- And, as a start-up in 2006, built a client base worth over £800,000 with average fees of £5,600 per client

So why have they been so willing to share their "success secrets", warts and all, so openly? And won't doing so damage their competitive advantage?

There seem to be four parts to the answer.

Firstly, they believe that there are more than enough clients, work and opportunities to go around.

Secondly, they recognise that the better the profession as a whole becomes, the better it is for everybody in the profession. Thus it is in their best long term interests if the entire profession succeeds along with them.

Thirdly, they suspect that many of the people who read this book will "fail to implement", so the actual competitive threat from others copying them is actually less than it should be. (The challenge to you, therefore, is to make sure that you don't fall into the trap of failing to implement).

And fourthly, they do not intend to stand still. So what you read on these pages is only their story so far. There is much more still to come.

About the firms featured in this book

The Examples of Excellence come from just about every corner of the United Kingdom. From Scotland to the West Country, and from village greens to city centres.

They also represent firms of all ages, from start-ups to long established practices, who can trace their roots back to the 19th Century. With partners and directors ranging from fresh faced 'twenty-somethings' to those in their sixties.

And they represent firms in all sorts of conditions and shape, from those facing the most extreme types of adversity, to those for whom life was already really good before they started making it even better.

Most importantly of all, perhaps, they represent independent accountancy firms of all sizes:

- 23 are sole practitioners
- Nine are two partner/director practices
- Four have three to five partners/directors
- Five have six or more partners/directors, including one with 16
- Of these, three are start-ups

Many of these are also firms that I have had the privilege of working with personally. Ultimately that proved inevitable, since, despite me writing to thousands of other accounting firms with whom I don't work, and inviting them to nominate themselves to be featured in this book, very few of them were willing to put their heads above the parapet.

For some this was presumably because they did not feel they were worthy of inclusion, or the time-frame wasn't right. While others were probably not willing to be candid and detailed enough in their explanation of what makes them special.

As a result, no doubt there are other firms worthy of inclusion, but for obvious reasons I have only been able to write about those who accepted my invitation.

There are also some firms who did accept the invitation, but due to space constraints and printing deadlines for these pages, didn't quite make the cut. They are unquestionably examples of excellence too. So one day I hope to be able to able to include them in a companion volume.

In the meantime, I am honoured that some of the firms featured, have chosen to specifically mention me or my business as being of help to them on their journey to excellence. However I know that, in reality, I have learned far more from them than they have ever learned from me.

What makes these firms the best?

Other research shows that in the UK many clients are unhappy with the service they receive from their accountants, and over half of all practitioners make an economic loss.

On the following pages you will read hundreds of practical and proven examples of how real practitioners are overcoming both of those challenges.

You will not find any theory. And you will also find very little commentary from me. That is deliberate, since I want the practitioners and their successes to speak for themselves. However, I do believe it is appropriate for me to summarise what are undoubtedly the key common themes across the case studies as a whole.

Therefore, in that spirit, I would like to suggest that the UK's best accountancy practices have:

1. **Better intent** – They don't make excuses or moan about what the world is doing to them. Instead they take control of their own destiny. Their success is planned and not accidental. They decide what they want, make whatever changes are necessary to ensure that they get it, and persevere when the going gets tough.

2. **Better decision making** – They make conscious, rational decisions, driven by their goals, and informed by facts rather than guesswork or pre-judgement. They do not run away from the need to invest time and money in creating success for them and their clients.

3. **Better measurement systems** – They don't just rely on traditional accounting measures. Instead they work out what really matters – i.e. what drives their success – both financial and non financial. They find ways of measuring all those success drivers, set targets, use the results to inform decision making and make people transparently accountable for performance and results.

4. **Better action** – They recognise that one of the timeless keys to success is to do what you said you were going to do, when you said you were going to do it. So they have systems to ensure that action plans are created, recorded, prioritised and implemented. And they do not accept lip service, excuses or weasel words.

5. **Better measurement solutions for clients** – They also recognise that profits are a consequence of doing the right things for the right people in the right way. So they start by making sure that their clients also get all the information they need about the numbers that really matter within their businesses, including their success drivers and benchmarking comparisons.

6. **Better improvement solutions for clients** – As well as helping clients to measure the things that matter, they also help them create and implement improvement action plans in those areas. In particular, they help clients create and implement improvement action plans for their profit, cashflow, tax exposure, business value and personal wealth.

7. **Better alliances** – They recognise that it is impossible for any independent accountancy firm to be able to do every specialist piece of work to the incredibly high standard that clients deserve. So they enter into strategic alliances with other specialists who will do the specialist technical work where necessary. Generally, the specialist takes all the engagement risk, and shares the fees generated with the practice in the form of a 'payaway'.

8. **Better client meetings** – They recognise that meetings are the equivalent of a penalty shoot out in a football tournament – i.e. the interaction that makes a profound difference to the outcome and how you are judged. So they make them more professional and dynamic by following carefully planned meeting systems, and using high impact tools, such as tax planning software, "live" at meetings to illustrate key ideas and quantify potential benefits.

9. **Better proactivity** – For them "proactivity" is not an empty promise on their website and in their brochure. They have developed systems to ensure that genuine proactivity, of the kind clients really value, is part of the culture and habits of the firm. They have also discovered that the more proactive they are, the more additional services their clients want to buy from them.

10. **Better service** – They understand what excellent service means to the type of clients they want to attract, and have focused their energy and designed their systems in order to deliver that. They focus on both the substance of service excellence (e.g. speed, accuracy, impact etc) and on the experiential aspect (e.g. showing genuine interest, using Plain English, 'wow factors' etc).

11. **Better clients** – They understand that their time is a precious commodity, so they ration it wisely. Rather than try to please every conceivable type of client, they decide the types of clients they really want to work with, and build the practice around them. That way, they attract more of the right kind of clients, and can afford to get rid of the

'wrong' kind of clients. Typically, this results in them earning more money, doing more enjoyable work, and having a better life-work balance by working with a smaller number of clients, paying higher average fees.

12. **Better pricing and cash management** – They recognise that the only sustainable way to provide a premium service is to charge a premium fee. They understand that clients hate surprise bills, and so rarely use timesheets for billing purposes. They also understand that, to clients, every bill is a value bill, since the client will not be happy unless it represents good value. So, wherever possible they use value pricing to make it crystal clear that the value far exceeds the fee. And where value pricing is not possible, they use pricing software to generate fixed prices that are acceptable to the client, and fixed price agreements to formalise the arrangement. They also use Extra Work Orders to ensure that extra work is translated into extra fees. And they collect most of their fees by direct debit, often by instalments and usually in advance of completing the work.

13. **Better team work** – They understand that the partners cannot and should not try to do everything. They recognise that leverageable success comes by fully involving the team at every stage. Listening to them properly, and valuing their input. Sharing all the key numbers with them. Trusting them. Delegating most of the work to them, after first giving them the tools, training, systems and support they need to do a proper job. And treating and rewarding them well.

14. **Better systems** – They do not leave things to chance, and they do not rely on their people remembering what to do. Instead, they create systems to ensure that everything can be done to the same high standard, every single time.

15. **Better marketing** – They do not leave referrals to chance. Instead, they use referral systems that leverage their time. They don't just look to clients and bank managers for referrals, they actively cultivate a much wider network of referral sources. And they understand that in order to get people telling others about them, they have to create a game the client wants to play, and give them a compelling story to tell. They also test a wide variety of other marketing strategies to find the ones that work best for them. For example, many of them have found that the right kind of seminars, are one of the best ways to win new clients.

By the way, if at the moment some of these success factors seem a little vague, relax. They will all make perfect sense once you have read the pages that follow, I promise!

How to use this book

The examples of excellence are presented in alphabetical order of firm name. As a result, there is no logic to its running order, and therefore you can either read it cover to cover, or can dip in and out wherever you like.

My advice, however, is as follows:

- Whatever order you decide to read it in, do make sure you read it all. There are so many powerful insights littered across the pages that you really can't afford to miss any of them

- Treat it as a work book rather than a library book – use a highlighter pen to identify the bits that resonate most with you, and annotate your thoughts in the margins

- Draw up a list of potential actions as you go along

- Share the book and your thoughts with the other key people in your practice

- Have a meeting to work out what you are going to do as a result of the book

- Draw up an action plan – with complete clarity over who is responsible for each action, and the date by which it must be done

- Give someone the job of holding you accountable to make sure that the things on your action plan are actually completed

As Ralph Thoburn says later in the book "None of us will ever come up with all the best ideas ourselves, and we shouldn't even try."

Happily, of course, you don't have to try to come up with ideas yourself, since on the following pages there are hundreds that have already been proven to work by firms just like yours. So don't try to reinvent the wheel. Instead use wheels that are already working.

Free implementation training and resources

To help you further, in Appendix 5 you will find details of the free implementation training and resources I have created for you. They include:

- a diagnostic tool to help you to decide where to focus your efforts,

- an action planning tool for formulating and prioritising an action plan that will get you results, and

- an invitation to spend a day with me on one of my seminars.

In addition, if you want to talk to any of the firms featured in this book, please email me at steve.pipe@avn.co.uk and I will send you a list containing the contact details of all those firms who are willing to discuss their successes with you.

The research process

I have been working as an adviser to the UK accountancy profession since 1998. So in one sense, the research for this book goes back to then.

But two years ago, in 2009, I started the formal process of identifying examples of excellence specifically for inclusion. Whatever works well for real UK practices in the worst recession of our lifetimes, I said to myself, will no doubt work well at any time. So it must be worth sharing with the rest of the profession.

The research process used was as follows:

- I wrote directly to thousands of accountants inviting them to participate, placed open invitations to the profession on forums such as accountingweb, and asked other advisers to nominate firms they felt were worthy of inclusion

- Firms told me their stories

- I wrote those stories up in draft form

- Each draft was then reviewed by the firm in question, amended and corrected by them as necessary, confirmed by them as a true and fair account, and approved by them for publication

All of the stories relate specifically to the things that have worked extraordinarily well over the last few years, and all of them have been written up in the last two years.

They are also all true and fair accounts of the situation at the time they were originally written. And some, but not all, have also been updated for additional developments to the Spring of 2011.

Two further explanations

There were two things I initially struggled with when writing this book.

The first was how to handle the fact that a number of the firms do some of the same things as each other. In the end I decided not to try to edit out any resulting repetition, since to do so would not have given a true account of what was driving each firm's success.

So where you see similar things being done by several firms, take extra notice, since those are the things that have the greatest weight of evidence behind them. They may therefore also be the things you should implement first in your firm.

The second thing I initially struggled with was whether to suppress the fact that some of the firms specifically mention tools created by my business, AVN, as being an important component of their success.

In the end, while I did indeed delete many such references, I also left others in on the basis that they were integral to the story, true to the reality, and were balanced by the fact that the book also contains references to the products and services of 21 other organisations that the best practice firms also found useful.

You can find a full list of all of these products and services in Appendix 2.

And, as they say, other useful tools are also available from other suppliers.

And now for all the excuses…

As a Chartered Accountant myself, married to an accountant, and having spent most of my life working with accountants, I know that the profession loves to find excuses why it doesn't need to change after all.

So, to make the profession's life easier in this respect, here is a comprehensive list of the excuses I normally hear, along with the reasons why no true professional can use them about the content of this book:

- **"It won't work / That is impossible"** – Every single idea in this book has been proved to work in the UK by a UK accountancy practice. That is the whole point.

- **"It won't work in our part of the country"** – The ideas have been proven to work by firms in every corner of the UK, from North to South, East to West, and village green to city centre.

- **"It won't work for a firm of our size"** – The ideas have also been proven to work by firms of all sizes, including three starts ups, 23 sole practitioners, 13 with two to five partners, and five with six or more partners.

- **"Our clients are different"** – In what way exactly? Do they not want better service, bigger profits, lower tax bills etc?

- **"Our firm is different"** – Of course it is. But so is every firm in this book. If they can change things for the better, so can you. In fact, you are the only people who can make your firm better. And the only question that matters is not whether you can, but whether you will?

- **"We are not good enough"** – Rubbish. If you are a professional, you are good enough. And if you are not a professional, you should not be in practice. As Ian Williams candidly puts it, in Example of Excellence 12, "I would describe myself as ordinary and of average ability. But I am passionate about doing the right things for clients, and that is what really counts. So if I can do it, anyone can."

- **"We would lose all of our clients if we put our prices up"** – No practitioner since the beginning of time has ever lost all of their clients in this way. But, of course, you may lose some clients. So the question that really matters is, will enough of your clients stay at your new prices? Happily, all the evidence in the book suggests that firms lose very few clients when they charge more, and fewer still of their good clients leave. And, of course, you want to lose some of your most price sensitive clients, since that is how you free up the time to serve your remaining clients better, and have a better life-work balance for yourself.

- **"We don't have the right type of clients"** – You are either right or wrong with this assertion. If you are wrong, then you have no excuse! And if you are right, and you really do have low-grade clients, consider what that is telling you: i.e. what you are currently doing is only good enough to attract low grade clients to your firm. If you are happy with only having low grade clients, fine. But if you would prefer to have better quality clients, then your only logical option is to change what you do in order to become more attractive to better clients.

- **"There are some other important things we need to do first"** – What could possibly be more important than serving clients better, and generating better results for you and your family? Certainly not redecorating the office, redesigning the website, installing new cabling and all the other similar excuses that other firms make for doing nothing.

- **"We will do it, but not now"** – The brutal truth is, you are kidding yourself. If you put off acting on the ideas in the book 'for now', you are in reality putting them off forever, since the half life of enthusiasm is short and there will always be other "more important" things in your in-tray.

- **"We tried that once and it didn't work"** – Logically, negative examples don't really prove anything. For example, if I were to pick up a Stradivarius violin and try to play it, sadly you would not hear sweet music. But just because I can't get it to work, doesn't prove that it doesn't work. In fact, all it proves is that I haven't currently acquired the skills and knowledge to make it work. Everything in this book has been proven to work by accountants just like you. So all you have to do is acquire the skills and knowledge to make them work for you too.

- **"We don't have the tools, skills or knowledge"** – Well get them then! They aren't difficult to obtain, and the examples of excellence and the resource list in Appendix 2 will point you very clearly in the right direction.

The challenge to accountants

When you follow in the footsteps of the UK's best accountancy firms, your results will get better. Lives will be made better too.

The lives of your clients, colleagues and team members.

Your life. And, perhaps even more importantly, the lives of your family and loved ones.

Since the more financially successful your practice is, the more there will be in the pot to pay for all the things you want to do with your family and loved ones, and for them.

While the less time consuming and stressful your practice is to run, the healthier and happier you will be, and the more time you will have to spend with your family and on all the other things that are important to you.

So, as an accountant and as a human being, you have a professional and moral duty not to let any of those people down.

And that means that once you know what is possible, you must do it.

Some of the key lessons the best firms have learned

The Examples of Excellence are crammed with invaluable insights, facts and figures, and detailed step-by-step "how to" guides that will no doubt monopolise your attention.

To me, however, some of the most valuable parts of the book are the lessons that the firms have learned on their journey. In this short chapter I have therefore drawn together a small selection of what I believe to be the most insightful quotes from partners in the featured firms.

Not only do they set the scene for the rest of the book, but they also contain some major clues as to what you should (and should not) do if you really want to become more successful.

> "The profoundly powerful and liberating truth we have discovered is this... by focussing on doing the right things for your clients and your team, you automatically start to get the profit and financial gain as a natural by- product. Putting it another way, profits are a consequence."
>
> *Ashley Barrowclough, Balance Accountants*

> "Our profession is woefully letting down its clients by not keeping pace with their needs and demands... The key is to look forward. To help them create a much better future. With much better profits. Much better cashflow. Much better tax bills. And much better wealth."
>
> *Mark Hollyman, ISIS*

> "Accountants have a moral and professional duty to ensure that their clients don't miss out on what is rightfully theirs."
>
> *David Scott, David Scott & Co*

> "By forming strategic alliances with specialists who will share their fees with you, you get the best of all worlds: first class solutions and service for your clients, highly profitable income for the practice, and all with less effort and engagement risk than if you did the work yourself."
>
> *Ian Williams, Elite Tax and Business Solutions*

"The most important thing an accountant can do is help a client identify and articulate what they really want out of their business and their life, and then help them to achieve it. That's the way we really make a difference. Ultimately it is about being in partnership with your clients, and not merely having a transactional sales ledger / purchase ledger relationship with them."

Rob Walsh, Clear Vision

"Regular meetings are essential to really understanding clients, building relationships and delivering value. And we find people who are serious about their businesses are really happy to pay for the additional value this gives them."

Peter Czapp, The Wow Company

"We are finding that, across the board, being more systematically proactive than ever before is creating a mountain of extra work (and profitable extra fees) for us."

Nino Pucacco, P & A Accountancy Services

"It is difficult to preach to clients about how they should run their businesses if you aren't doing the same with your own business."

Ashley Barrowclough, Balance Accountants

"The difference a good accountant can make is profound."

Rob Walsh, Clear Vision

"Our experience is that when you serve clients properly, and explain the situation carefully, fee resistance melts away."

Alan Cowperthwaite, Harvey Smith & Co

"What we have found is that price resistance melts away when you do the right things. So my belief is that price resistance is self inflicted pain – i.e. something that firms meet when they are not doing enough of the right things for clients."

Mark Hollyman, ISIS

"Now I realise that clients are happy to pay high fees when the benefits are far higher still."

Jo Sole, Sole Associates

"Of course we don't appeal to people who are treading water between jobs, price shoppers, timewasters and carrier bag jobs, but who cares? Those are not the kind of clients we want anyway, and I can tell you that life is so much more enjoyable without them."

Ian Main, Stark Main

"Every entrepreneur knows that you have to speculate to accumulate, and invest in order to earn a return."

Paul Meades, Meades & Co

"If you really want to do something, but your partners aren't yet convinced, find a mutually agreeable way of giving it a go within your sphere of influence. After all, it is your life, and it is not right for other people's agendas, beliefs and prejudices to stop you living it to the full."

Ian Williams, Elite Tax and Business Solutions

"Once I became really committed to change I started reaping the benefits, and am now enjoying both my business and my life much more as a result. Having turned 60, I only wish I had started changing sooner!"

Keith Anderson, Anderson Advantage

"I would describe myself as ordinary and of average ability. But I am passionate about doing the right things for clients, and that is what really counts. So if I can do it, anyone can."

Ian Williams, Elite Tax and Business Solutions

"All simple and obvious stuff really, but doing it all properly has made a huge difference."

Ashley Barrowclough, Balance Accountants

Modern management, meetings and measurement systems lead to £7.6 million in tax savings for clients

In 2009 this two partner practice from Cambuslang, near Glasgow, was facing three challenges:

- The news that one of the two partners wanted to retire, which meant the old ways of working were no longer viable

- The fact that the economy had officially entered the worst recession for over 50 years, which meant continuing in business could not be taken for granted

- A recognition of the need to provide "sensational service" that had a tangibly positive impact on clients' bank accounts, since the alternative was seeing clients switching to cheaper accountants, or perhaps even going out of business

By implementing four main changes, the firm was not only able to overcome these challenges, but also make great strides in improving its fee base, profitability, and cashflow, as well as greatly improving job satisfaction and career prospects for everyone at the firm.

Non-retiring partner Matt Donnelly comments "Our average fees are now £2,797 per client, which when you remove the effect of a significant reduction in revenues from one major client, represents a healthy increase. In the present economic climate we are delighted to have maintained our market share and to have been able to reward our management team for their success."

The four key changes they made, were to introduce:

1. A modern management structure

2. Modern meeting arrangements

3. Modern measurement systems, and

4. A modern approach to tax planning

Modern management structure

Historically, as at many firms, the two partners had been the key people in the practice: they were clients' main point of contact, they "owned" client relationships, they were the only people who knew the full facts about how well the practice was doing, they made most of the decisions and, as a result, they had to work really long hours in order to get everything done.

According to Matt Donnelly: "When 50% of partner time was about to be taken out of the equation, that old way of working was no longer an option, since I would have probably killed myself trying to do the work of two partners. And it would also have been impossible to grow the firm. So instead we decided to adopt a fundamentally different management structure that has worked superbly well."

Under the new structure Matt no longer takes any active part in planning, controlling or actually doing any of the technical work within the business. All of that is now done by a leadership team of four managers, who in turn are supported by 14 other employees. The leadership team consists of the following:

1. **Production Co-ordination Manager** – who leads an accounts team and is responsible for production planning, scheduling and reviewing to ensure that all jobs are completed efficiently and effectively

2. **Tax Manager** – who leads a tax team that deals with day to day tax correspondence and compliance. This leaves the tax manager to concentrate on proactive tax planning for clients, tax investigation support and running seminars that help the firm to both win new clients and generate goodwill and additional fees from existing clients

3. **Finance and Administration Manager** – who leads the support team, with responsibilities that include IT, marketing and finance

4. **Production and Commercial Manager** – whose responsibilities include: carrying out Extra Work Order reviews on every job to make sure the firm bills for all work that is outside the scope of a Fixed Price Agreement; conducting annual business relationship reviews with every client to clarify the value of what the firm has already done for them, obtain feedback and referrals, and identify further ways in which the firm can help the client; and ensuring that the firm meets it cross selling targets.

As a result, Matt Donnelly now plays the role of a modern Managing Partner. "I am now able to concentrate on profitably growing the business and energy of ad+. Our chosen word for 2011 is "self control" in that we believe that appropriate organization, planning and control of ourselves and our actions will ultimately allow the business to grow in terms of profitability and energy."

Modern meeting arrangements

The next step was for the leadership team to design a three tier structure for daily, weekly and monthly meetings.

Daily routines:

- **'Huddle'** – Each of the teams meet to discuss the tasks for the day ahead and brainstorm any issues that need attention.

- **'Big rocks huddle'** – The leadership team meet to agree the major items which must be addressed in the day ahead which will drive the firm to achieve its One Page Plan targets (see next page).

- **'Commercial rocks huddle'** – Where the leadership team discusses how to make the most of all commercial activities that day, including meetings with clients and introducers.

Weekly routines:

- **Client relationship meeting** – all team members meet as a group every Friday morning to discuss the previous week's results and share any client news.

- **Leadership Team 'grow the people meeting'** – the managers meet every Friday afternoon to discuss: (a) people and management issues that have arisen, (b) other issues and opportunities that have arisen, (c) holding each other accountable for progress on agreed actions, and (d) what else the firm can do in order to achieve its One Page Plan targets.

- **Commercial meeting** – where potential leads and business development opportunities are discussed with the managing partner.

Monthly Routines:

- **Production review** – held on the first day of each month. At this meeting the production team reviews their results from the month before, documents any lessons learnt from jobs completed, and updates and improves their systems accordingly.

- **Sales opportunity preview** – in the third week the managers meet to discuss the workflow for the coming month and use this as an opportunity to review clients' additional needs and potential cross selling opportunities.

- **Leadership Team Meeting** – this meeting focuses on assessing the performance of the leadership team, holding each other accountable for progress on agreed actions, reiterating the One Page Plan targets and desired outcomes for the year, refining and improving the strategy for achieving those plans, and updating the action plan.

"This may sounds like a lot of meetings," says Matt. "But I can tell you for a fact, investing a small amount of time in them pays huge dividends. It brings focus, discipline and accountability. It helps the team by improving communication and makes them feel more valued. It helps clients by improving service levels and turnaround times, and by giving us more of the up-to-the-minute information we need to be more proactive. And it helps the firm by reducing mistakes, enhancing efficiency, improving decision making and getting us to take more action by making us more accountable."

"So the benefits are immense. And by using carefully designed agendas for each meeting we also keep the time cost down to much less than you might expect."

Modern measurement systems

The other key to making the new leadership and meeting arrangements work, is that the firm sets targets for everything that matters, and systematically measures actual performance against those targets on a One Page Plan. (The One Page Plan is a goal based measurement, target setting, action planning and control system for managing a business using a single A4 sheet of paper).

"We have a One Page Plan for the firm as a whole, as well as for each department," explains Matt. "Together they are by far the most important documents within our business. They are referred to at just about every meeting because they constantly remind us of what we are trying to achieve, show us how well we are doing, and help us work out how to do even better. They therefore keep our meetings and our decisions rooted in facts not guesswork. And that leads to better accountability, better decisions and better results."

Finance and Administration Manager Angela McKendrick puts it this way: "The One Page Plan is our daily 'truth report', constantly checking each of us in the leadership team to ensure that we are on track to deliver on the firm's targets and goals."

Some of the things measured on the firm's One Page Plan include:

- Average team satisfaction score on a scale of 1-10
- Number of jobs completed, issued and invoiced
- Number of face to face meetings with clients
- Average customer satisfaction score
- Value of extra work orders from existing clients
- Number of meetings with influencers
- Number of new sales leads added to the "pipeline"

- Number of live sales in the pipeline

- Number of first and second meetings with potential clients

- Number and value of new clients signed up

Modern approach to tax planning

As part of their determination to provide "sensational service" that has a tangibly positive impact on clients' bank accounts, the firm decided to become much more proactive with tax planning and minimisation.

This manifested itself in the tax team:

- Setting a target of saving clients an extra £1 million in tax in 2010

- Creating a system to achieve those savings by proactively reviewing the tax planning opportunities for every client and every project (remember, the new team structure meant that the tax manager had been freed from day to day involvement in tax correspondence and compliance in order to be able to focus on exactly this kind of proactive tax work)

- Forming strategic alliances with third party tax planners who can provide specialist leading-edge tax planning solutions that are inevitably beyond the technical expertise of general practitioners

- Systematically quantifying the tax savings ultimately obtained, no matter how small or large.

As a result of launching this approach they saved 61 clients an extra £7.6 million in tax in 2010. The savings came from a wide variety of situations, including clearing overdrawn directors' loan accounts, preventing VAT mistakes and penalties, reducing corporation tax exposure, and becoming better at defending clients from the taxman's attempts to persuade them to pay a lot more tax than they need to. For example, defending clients from CIS status challenges has become a real success story for the firm: in 2010 they achieved a 100% success rate for clients and even saved one client just over £909,000 in PAYE and NIC.

Matt Donnelly explains: "Of course, saving clients £7.6 million in tax is extremely rewarding financially and professionally for the firm. But much more importantly, it is also incredibly valuable to our clients. In fact to some of them it has probably made the difference between surviving the recession and being taken under by it."

He added, "We were always good at tax planning. But setting a target for it, and creating the right systems, structure and strategic alliances have created the focus to ensure that we are now truly proactively excellent at it. And proactive excellence is what clients deserve, it's what they will gladly pay good money for, and it is the reason they are now referring more people to us."

Doubling turnover and taking Fridays off

Based in Redruth, Cornwall, sole practitioner Keith Anderson of Anderson Advantage has doubled his turnover in less than eighteen months, and also stopped working on Fridays.

Achieving growth through qualified resources

The start of the growth process, strange as it may sound at first, involved getting rid of a junior member of staff. However, this was a positive strategy that saw the junior replaced by a fully qualified accountant. "He was given the specific task of looking after all the compliance work in the office," explains Keith. "So, since February 2010, I have not touched a set of accounts or a single tax return. I even had some time off in January 2011. And since he took over the control of this, it has enabled me to implement Michael Gerber's mantra of working on my business not in it."

"Another wonderful consequence is that I now take Friday's off," added Keith. Working on the business meant getting more jobs in and having the resources available to provide the required level of service. The first step was to appoint a telemarketing company that contacted prospective clients and arranged interviews with them. This meant that Keith "went about doing the job I really enjoy – meeting new clients. All I would carry with me at the appointed time was a laptop with some software packages."

Demonstrating capability to prospective clients

The three software packages he demonstrated to prospective clients were:

- Incorporation Tax Planner to be able to show sole traders and partners how much tax they could save by incorporating

- Remuneration Tax Planner to indicate the amount of tax companies could save by extracting their profits tax efficiently

- Times Up pricing software to calculate instantly how much Anderson's services would cost the client.

"These three programmes enabled me to show a very high level of sophistication and professional ability," comments Keith. "I was immediately able to show clients tax savings, which is what people are interested in. I was also able to quote a fixed fee at the meeting, which the potential client agreed to whilst we were together."

He also improved his service offering by:

- Including tax investigation insurance at no extra charge

- Offering free telephone contact with any of his team between the hours of 8am and 10pm

- Expanding his guarantee so that if he doesn't produce a client's accounts within 30 working days of receiving all the information, then he rebates 50% of the fee

"Taken together these changes have really worked, as new clients have been signing up with us at prices higher, and in some cases 100% higher, than what their existing accountants were charging."

Impressing clients with a professional image

The increased selling effort was accompanied by a change of image, in terms of personal appearance and the car driven, in an effort to impress prospective clients. Keith remarks: "I went back to the full suit, white shirt, loud tie, cufflinks and clean shoes. In addition, I changed my car from a Honda to a Jaguar XF. These personal details are important as they give an appearance of professionalism and success. Many clients have said that 'if you can afford to buy a car like that, you must be good'."

Lasting benefits

Once the initial round of marketing and selling was complete, the telemarketing contract was terminated at the end of 2010, having achieved the required aims. However, the benefits of the campaign are, Keith confirms, still being felt: "2011 has already seen us add over thirty new clients paying combined fixed fees of £50,000. And when you consider that Cornwall is made up of mostly small, one-man band businesses, the average fee is very high. Most of these new clients have come from referrals from existing clients."

And since a significant proportion of the accounts preparation work has been outsourced, the practice is easily able to handle the extra work and has no worries about further growth.

The dramatic increase in his fee base is not, he insists, a short-term phenomenon: "Most of my turnover is paid by standing order with signed fixed fee agreements so I know what to expect in the next six months."

Why revolution is better than evolution

West Yorkshire based Balance Accountants is a one partner and 15 team member practice that is reaping huge financial and personal benefits by rebranding, reinventing and reinvigorating themselves. In this section, the firm's principal, Ashley Barrowclough explains in his own words exactly how they did it.

The challenge

By the end of 2008 our turnover was around £750,000, but in the second half of 2009 the recession began to bite, work slowed down, cash flow slowed down and it became clear that we were overstaffed. Morale was also low and we knew that changes had to be made.

We had two options available to us – Evolution or Revolution. So we opted for the latter, and attacked the problem in two ways. Firstly, by rebranding. And secondly, by improving our systems and the way we measure things.

And by seeing those two changes through, as I write this in early 2011:

- Our people are excited, positive, motivated and happier than ever before
- Our clients love the changes, and are buying more added value services than ever before
- Our financial results have been transformed
- The practice is growing rapidly
- And we no longer fear the recession

The rebranding process

We had always believed ourselves to be different (in a good way) from other accountants in the area. But our trading name of "Rogers & Co Chartered Accountants" didn't portray this. Neither did our logo, letterhead or offices.

So we sat down with an outside consultant and a design agency and created Balance Accountants; a new trading name and brand that we could be proud of, that we could identify with and that represented our culture. We believe the new brand is modern, vibrant, trendy and different (you can judge for yourself by looking at www.balanceonline.co.uk).

But a brand is not just a new name and a logo; it has to represent what the firm is all about and it has to be supported by substance in terms of the products and services that we offer, and the attitude of the people who have to roll it out. So our whole team was involved in the process. It was the team that decided upon Revolution over Evolution. It was the team that chose the design consultants to work with. And it was the team that chose the name, colours, logo and stationery.

New products and services to match the brand

With a new, modern and vibrant brand identity, we needed to focus on products and services that matched. It was no use trying to push our new image by rolling out the same old compliance services. So we decided to focus on three new services:

1. **"The Numbers"** – A folder containing a complete performance measurement and improvement system that gives clients their finger on the pulse of every number that really matters in their business, so they have the information and insights they need to make better decisions and get better results.

2. **"BoardView"** – This is where we get paid to meet with clients on a quarterly basis to review their performance, act as a sounding board, help with problem solving, share insights, give advice, and explore opportunities for growth and putting them on the fast track to wherever it is they want to go.

3. **"Virtual FD"** – Which gives clients all the benefits of having a Financial Director on their side, without exposing themselves to all the complications, risks and drawbacks of actually employing one. And has a high price tag that reflects its value.

We now give The Numbers folders to all A & B category clients. The cost of BoardView is automatically built into our quotes for all new clients, and is also being cross-sold as an optional extra to existing clients. And The Virtual FD service is kept in reserve for those clients who need even more help.

New tangibles to match the brand

Visually our new brand is based on a very distinctively memorable "Balance yellow" colour that is far removed from the conservative colours usually associated with accountants.

Some of the ways we have made the new brand central to the experience of visiting and working with us include:

*   High quality Balance yellow branded crockery
*   A range of Balance yellow branded brochures and leaflets

- Presenting The Numbers in striking Balance yellow branded folders
- Major building work to make the office more stylish and functional
- And boldly branding the remodelled office by painting some of the walls Balance yellow (we carefully chose the walls so that they contrasted stylishly with the neighbouring more neutral coloured walls) and featuring huge versions of the "Balance – Accountants for growth" logo and slogan

The result is a colourful and vibrant environment, which not only draws many positive comments from visitors, but also makes us proud.

A new digital presence to match the brand

For many years we had been using a "template website" which served its purpose at the time, but did not do justice to our new image. So we had a brand new website developed which focuses on our team, since ultimately it is our people that make us special, our people who serve our clients and our people who make the difference.

It still talks about our main services, of course. But it does so in a brief and eye-catching way. And it humanises everything by featuring quirky photographs of the team doing things they love, showing us as approachable and likeable human beings with a healthy dose of personality, and making it impossible for people to assume that we are staid and stuffy professionals. It re-emphasises this point by also containing fun and memorable animation, and banning all the predictable elements such as tax tables and the other dull and boring things that are frequently found on other accountants' websites.

So when people visit our website they instantly see that we are a practice with attitude and personality. If they find that a turn-off, great, since we clearly aren't right for each other. And it is far better to realise that before we meet, than waste a couple of hours meeting them, only then to reach the same conclusion. So it saves us time, energy and money too.

Promoting the new brand

The old Rogers & Co would have sat in the office doing compliance work, waiting for new clients to come to us.

The new Balance is out there networking, exhibiting, getting featured in newspapers and magazines, and generally getting ourselves known. But even here we do things a little differently. For example, at exhibitions we hand out bags of sweets with our business cards, which really gets us noticed. And we have also worked with Steve Pipe to produce our own business improvement book, with our name and logo on the cover, which really impresses people.

Systems and measurement improvements

This was not as exciting and obvious as the rebranding, but it was equally important. We felt that we never really had control of our business in the old Rogers & Co days. But we knew that had to change. Partly because it is essential for the success of our own business. And partly, because it is difficult to preach to clients about how they should run their businesses if you aren't doing the same with your own business, i.e. practising what you preach.

We now have much more comprehensive and detailed P & L and cash flow forecasts for the year ahead. The forecast turnover is predicted precisely because every single piece of client's work is factored into it. Of course the forecast changes as we pick up new clients, or one off assignments crop up, but by having this detail and flexing it for new/additional work, we know exactly what needs doing in every single month and what our staffing requirements are going to be. So our work planning and resource allocation is far more effective and efficient.

We also have detailed monthly management accounts tied in to our own one page plan so that we can measure, analyse and improve any facet of the business that needs it. And we have graphs for everything financial, which we share with the whole team.

In addition, we have also worked hard to create a slick, well monitored operational process that has been highly systemised so that it now runs day in day out without too much senior management involvement.

All simple and obvious stuff really, but doing it all properly has made a huge difference. In fact, taken together with the rebranding they have had a remarkable effect upon our business, our clients and our team.

Remarkable benefits

Within 6 months cash flow had improved and is now excellent – due in no small part to the fact that we also started using direct debits to get paid, and passed responsibility for debt collection to our client managers.

Turnover is hitting targets and profitability is significantly up. The team is really enjoying the work, jobs are turning round within our 30 day target time, and recoveries are averaging 107%.

What's more, all of this has been achieved at the same time as reducing our team from 21 to 15 people.

Even more remarkable benefits from rebranding

Of all the things we have done, it is the rebranding process which has produced the most significant results. Because of it we are picking up new clients, existing clients are buying additional services, people are talking about us, our clients love our new approach and the general atmosphere here at Balance is very, very optimistic. And all this is happening in the deepest recession for 70 years.

We are picking up high quality clients from our rebranded website – for example, a design agency whose previous accountants charged £600, are now paying us £4,200 for a bundle of services including BoardView.

We are picking up clients from Twitter – for example, a website design company in their first year of trading have also signed up at £4,200 for the bundle that includes BoardView.

And people are referring more clients to us than ever before – for example Business Link introduced us to a business, selling consumer goods on E Bay, that paid its previous accountants £100 a month and is now paying us £4,200, including BoardView. In fact, this business asked for references before signing up, and were overwhelmed by the positive response from the clients that they spoke to.

In addition, at least 10 of our existing clients having either already agreed to pay for our new BoardView service, or are on the cusp of doing so.

But it is not just BoardView that is working really well for us. For example, one client who used to pay us around £7,500 a year, is now paying £25,000 a year for our new Virtual FD service.

We set ourselves a target of £50k of net new business in the 12 months to 30 April 2011. And as I write this in early 2011 we have already passed that target with almost 4 months of our financial year still to go.

The most important benefit of all

For us there are two things that are even more valuable than the profits and financial gain the changes have brought us (although we welcome those things too!).

Our clients have been excited about the transformation. And we now have a really happy team.

In fact, the rebranding has inspired the team in a way that we could never have imagined – at a time when morale was low. We now have a loyal team, who are totally committed to the firm. They have bought into the brand. And they are 100% committed to what we are trying to achieve, and have become great ambassadors for the firm.

But the profoundly powerful and liberating truth we have discovered is this... by focusing on doing the right things for your clients and your team, you automatically start to get the profit and financial gain as a natural by-product.

Putting it another way, profits are a consequence.

Six month business improvement programme

Bartfields, a six director firm in Leeds, has successfully piloted a 'Business Improvement Programme' ('BIP') for its clients and prospects. And, having earned £12,600 from the first 4 businesses it has run it with, it is now poised to roll it out to the rest of its client base.

What the Business Improvement Programme is

The Bartfields BIP is a facilitated forum for groups of 4-6 business owners. Meeting half a day a month for six months, the forum is carefully designed to provide a fast track to realising business and personal success potential by:

- Having a short presentation (typically 20-60 minutes) on a key business topic at each meeting – e.g. the topics at the first six meetings were goals, prospering through the recession, exit strategy, marketing strategy, getting and keeping customers, and getting the best from your team.

- Spending most of the rest of the monthly meetings identifying the key challenges and problems each delegate faces, and using the collective insights and wisdom of the entire group to work out appropriate solutions.

- Ending each meeting with goal setting and action planning for the month ahead so that everyone was crystal clear what they needed to do to improve things in the areas discussed.

- Proactively phoning them between meetings to ensure they stay on track with their action plans.

- Being supportive, impartial and non judgemental at all times.

How it works

Director David Miller explains: "We priced the six month programme at £3,000 per business, but reduced that to £1,800 as a special offer for the pilot. And we also helped them to get £1,000 of the cost paid for by Train to Gain related funding for leadership and management training."

"In many ways the entire group acts as a sort of 'virtual board' for each other. For my part, I play the role of Virtual Finance Director, making sure that we never lose sight of the numbers. One of my colleagues acts as Virtual Managing Director, making sure we stay focused and effective. While the rest of the group act as general Virtual Directors, bringing their respective experience and skills to bear."

In fact the 'Virtual MD' is an associate of the firm who specialises in coaching owner managed businesses. "Running it in conjunction with an experienced business coach makes it so much better. Not only does it take the time pressure off my shoulders, but the specialist skills of a coach, including effective diagnostic questioning, helped to generate better results for its clients."

Results

The results make impressive reading:

- Four businesses initially signed up for the pilot programme so the practice earned £7,200 from that.

- Of the four, three found it so valuable that they asked Bartfields to run a second follow-up programme for their second-in-commands too. And at a further £1,800 each, that second programme generated another £5,400 in fees for the firm.

- The benefits weren't just restricted to the £12,600 in extra fees from the programme itself. The group members also asked us to provide extra help outside the BIP arrangement, including attending their board meetings and providing business growth ideas.

- Only two of the businesses that went through the programme were already clients. "The third was a large Independent Financial Advisor business we knew through the networking group BNI. So starting a paying relationship with them was a major coup."

- The process was extremely enjoyable for all concerned. David explained: "My fellow directors couldn't believe how much laughter they heard coming from the meeting room, which is a testament to the sorts of bonds and comfortableness that formed between group members. And for my part I can tell you that attending a BIP meeting is far more enjoyable and rewarding than reviewing a file!"

- One of the main lessons learned was not to pre-judge which clients would be interested. "Of the three we worked with, one was a client in his 70's from the construction industry. He is a very straight talking Yorkshireman, and there is no way we could have predicted his enthusiasm for the process. So if we had prejudged things we would never have invited him to take part, and both he and us would have lost out as a consequence."

David added: "Having used the pilot to learn how to make BIP a success, we are now planning a major seminar later in the year to formally launch it to the rest of our clients and contacts."

Referral lunches

The BIP also greatly strengthened the firm's referral relationship with the large IFA that participated. As a result they decided to launch a new referral system in conjunction with a solicitor and computer services company they also knew from BNI:

- Every month the four of them meet for lunch.

- But they must also bring along a guest from outside their firm – i.e. a client or contact.

- So they each meet three new prospects every month – and are given glowing endorsements by each other.

David explains "I leave most months with three strong referrals, which makes it both an extremely enjoyable and an extremely valuable way to spend a lunchtime."

How a small accountancy practice prospered in adverse conditions

At a time when many local practices have been working reduced hours or making redundancies, Plymouth based businessVision has prospered. In the year to June 2010 it increased its profitability by 64.9% without having to take on more staff. Indeed, the team now gets an extended weekend by finishing at 1:30 pm every Friday, as a result of extending the start and finish times on the other days so that they have worked 37 hours by Friday lunchtime.

Better working methods also mean that this sole practitioner, with a team of only eight members plus the principal, is managing to compete successfully with much bigger firms in the area.

So, how has all this been achieved? What is behind the improved fortunes? Quite simply, it's through a changed way of working that has allowed everyone to operate more effectively and provide a higher level of service to clients.

The practice has increasingly focused on serving its 'ideal client', replacing low value work with high turnover clients. This provides work that has not only resulted in the significant increase in profits, but is more interesting for the team as well.

Serving clients better

As part of the improved service, clients of businessVision now routinely receive extra information to help them understand their businesses better and make better decisions. For example:

- All clients receive a detailed 5 Year Trend Analysis report with their accounts

- All clients also receive a "What If ?" report that shows how much higher profits would be if the client could make small changes to its profit drivers

- And all clients get a "Where Did the Money Go?" layman's cash flow statement

- Most clients receive a Benchmarking report

- Most clients also receive a "Cash Wastage" report that illustrates the reasons for changes to their bank balances

- In 2009 many clients also received a "Beat the Recession" pack

- Many clients have a One Page Plan produced, either monthly or quarterly, which provides key performance indicators so they can keep track of what is happening.

- While those clients that are limited companies, also receive remuneration planning advice at least twice a year – with reviews carried out before the end of the tax year and at accounts follow-up meetings.

Better meetings too

But that is not all, as the principal Marc Lawson explains: "How well meetings go is one of the ways that clients judge us. So we make sure that our meetings always run smoothly by producing a written agenda for every meeting, creating a written action plan at the end of every meeting, and making sure that everything is discussed in plain English rather than confusing clients with jargon. And to help them run their own meetings better, we also offer them BoardView packs with practical guidance on how to run effective board meetings."

"As well as all these substantive aspects of excellent service we also work hard to make the experience of working with us a distinctively positive and memorable one. So, at meetings for example, we always reserve parking spaces for them (with their name actually on the reserved sign), if meetings run late our team will automatically offer to order them some sandwiches, and we also offer to answer their mobile phone to save them being interrupted unless it really is urgent. And it is those sort of little touches that clients really appreciate."

Helping clients through Signposting

The businessVision website has a "SignPosting" section, as Marc Lawson explains: "This is available to clients (and preferred suppliers) so that all of them can do business with each other in those areas where we can't help, and creates for us a far more profitable client base. Each SignPosting is linked to the client's own website, but there is the facility for users of their services/ products to answer a quick survey (of about 3 questions) that is fed back to us. This will then give us either a testimonial that we can pass onto the SignPosting client, or on rare occasions a complaint that we can then go through and use to improve the relevant systems in their organisation. Clients really find this valuable, and it really sets us apart from our competitors."

Business club

A significant activity for the practice is running its "Business Builder Forum" business club. These not only provide revenue from ticket sales, but also give significant benefit to clients and improve businessVision's reputation for supplying a professional service. The firm has been running Business Builder Forums since 2001 and completed its one hundredth event in July 2010, with many clients attending regularly.

According to Marc, "This has by far and away been the most successful professional action we have taken to help clients. Fees to attend have typically been £40 per month, and attendee numbers have ranged from about 20 per month to over 50 on some occasions. But income from ticket sales is only the start. The real payback comes from the way it has helped to build our reputation, get us more referrals, turn more prospects into clients and get clients buying additional services from us. That has been priceless."

Better marketing

Some of the ways businessVision is now marketing itself more effectively include:

- Creating a 4-page *"Why businesses choose businessVision"* report that sets out the practice's unique selling points
- Collecting testimonials from clients and putting them, together with press cuttings, in a folder on the reception table
- Giving potential and target clients a three-page summary of carefully selected testimonials

Improved pricing and better cash flow

As well as increasing and improving its range of services to clients, businessVision has altered its charging and payment arrangements. All fees are on a fixed price basis, calculated using pricing software, meaning that clients know exactly what they're going to pay and overcoming the perception that accountants don't have to rush because they're paid by the hour. Any extra work is quoted for separately using an "Extra Work Order", which has to be approved by the client before any extra work starts, and all recurring work is re-quoted annually to cover changed circumstances.

Turnaround times are guaranteed, such as 20 working days for accounts and seven days for tax returns, assuming no delays at the client's end. Added to this is an overall guarantee that clients will get quality and value that matches the fee they pay. If they don't think this is the case, they're entitled to pay any fee they think is appropriate, including nothing.

One thing they have done which has had a transformative effect on their cashflow is that the vast majority of clients now pay monthly by direct debit, often in advance of the work being done. This resulted in negative debtor days of -£160,703 at the last count – i.e. a net credit balance on their sales ledger.

As Marc Lawson says: "Having over £160k in prepaid fees has made a huge difference to our cashflow. And when you compound that with the fact that our fees are now also so much more profitable, things have never been better."

Helping themselves by working smarter

The practice's increased profitability and its ability to handle more business without having to take on more staff, is largely down to involving the entire team in finding ways to work smarter.

Two of the keys to this have been the firm's One Page Plan and System Builder software, as Marc Lawson explains: "The core of our success is our own One Page Plan which is completed monthly and presented to the team at our Monday morning meetings. We have been doing this for over 8 years and it is the single best thing we have ever done from a strategic point of view. It means that everyone knows what is important to the success of the practice, everyone knows we want them to help us achieve more in those important areas, and everyone sees the impact of their ideas and innovations as they show up in improved results the following month."

"The other key for us has been AVN's System Builder software, which is used by every single team member and is constantly open on their desktops. We've added hundreds (if not thousands) of our own systems and resources to it as we've gone along but still have some way to go. And as a result, at the push of a button it shows us exactly what to do in almost every conceivable situation. So we never have to reinvent the wheel, or make things up as we go along, since we always have proven best practice systems to follow. Which means we can give our clients better and quicker service, thereby driving up client loyalty at the same time as driving down our costs."

Aiming for future growth

Having achieved increases in turnover and profitability, businessVision does not intend to stand still.

The plan now is to continue to provide extra value for money to clients, not by reducing fees but rather by improving and increasing the range of services and advice. The intention is also to create greater awareness of what is available.

Perhaps a surprising target is that they aim to reduce the size of their client base to just 125 clients. However, this isn't as odd as it sounds. Focusing on fewer but bigger and better clients has proved to be a sound strategy over the previous twelve months and this is simply a continuation of that policy. Having fewer clients will mean that more time and attention can be devoted to each one, with a consequent increase in service and revenue.

Other specific items on the agenda for the next twelve months include:

- A client concierge system so that clients are automatically contacted on a regular basis – with the frequency of contact being determined by their client rating system

- Producing an MOT type checklist of the common issues, problem areas and opportunities that arise when they review clients' accounts and tax affairs – and presenting their finding to clients in an MOT style report

- Uploading and downloading of client documents through a secure web portal and providing electronic document storage for clients

- Conducting an online survey of key clients to improve the practice's knowledge of their clients' situation and needs, so that they can more fully serve those needs

- Introducing a fast track booking in system so that work on accounts can start promptly.

The overall aim is to provide a more comprehensive service, with greater clarity, so that businessVision will become a key part of each client's operation. As a result, the practice expects to see further increases in turnover and profitability.

How an established firm with a previously stagnant fee base achieved 28% and 21% fee growth in the last two years

Nick Hume runs the Ashford office of Kent based Calcutt Matthews. Started in 1999, the office now has a team of 6 people and c. 250 clients. Excluding the first couple of years when high percentage growth rates were almost inevitable, the annual growth rate had never been more than 7%. But two years ago it jumped to 21%, and last year rose further to 28% despite the economy being in the grip of the worst recession for 50 years.

Explaining the transformation in the office's fortunes, Nick said:

"While the number of clients has increased, it is the improvement in the quality of the client base that has been most pleasing. For example, in the last 6 weeks alone we have picked up four new clients all in the £7-8,000 annual recurring fee range, and they aren't even included in our 28% growth for last year. So compared to the past we are massively overachieving, and I personally have never been happier."

The six keys to 28% annual growth

Digging deeper, six of the most important factors behind his success are clearly:

1. He has complete clarity over his goal

2. He uses his bonus system very carefully to align his team to that goal

3. He turns some clients away

4. He uses Train To Gain funding in a very innovative way

5. He has set up a number of really innovative strategic alliances

6. And he gives banks a really strong reason to refer work to the practice

It all starts with a clear goal

Nick's goal is to build a practice with 100 proper business clients (at the moment he has just over 60, with the rest of his 250 clients being made up of the usual selection of tax return only, not for profit, and lifestyle businesses etc).

Those 100 clients will pay average fees of £10,000 each for an extended range of services that will include traditional accounting, advanced tax planning and business advice. Some will pay more than £10,000, others less, but in total they will generate £1m in recurring fees.

And those 100 clients will be served by a team of five "client managers" – i.e. senior professionals who each manage a portfolio of 20 clients, generating fees of £200,000. With only 20 clients to serve each, the client managers will be able to develop genuine expertise in their industries and businesses, and deep relationships with each client. This will ensure that the service is of the highest personal and professional standard.

Nick's role will be to overview the work of the client managers, ensuring that the service level really is excellent, and getting involved in the small proportion of issues that really do warrant input from the top man.

Clearly this goal is not something that will happen by itself. So Nick is developing a very clear action plan to make it a reality – and every decision he takes is made in the context of "what do we need to do here to ensure that we achieve our goal?"

A bonus system that actually works

The overall goal of becoming a £1m practice allows Nick to set annual target fee levels. And this in turn allows him to set monthly target fee levels. His bonus scheme then pays out the following amounts:

- Every month where the actual fees raised exceed the target level for the month, 10% of the surplus is paid over to the team as a bonus (that way the team members are rewarded quickly for hitting targets, and this instant gratification element makes them all the more determined to achieve the same feat the next month).

- Each December the actual fees for the year are compared to the target, and an extra payment is made, to bring the total bonus the team receives, up to 30% of the surplus.

To some practitioners paying a 30% bonus may sound like heresy. But actually it makes perfect commercial sense. Remember, the target level Nick sets already reflects the need to pay all his overheads, and pay him his target level of profits and keep the firm on track toward its ultimate goal. So because the bonus only starts to pay out once that target is reached, he is already getting everything he had hoped for, and paying the bonus is something he is actually very keen to do since it means that the business is actually doing even better than he had hoped, so everybody wins and everybody is happy.

Turning some clients away

Nick has realised that his time is a scarce and precious resource – and that he cannot afford to fritter it away on any Tom, Dick or Harry that comes through the door. So he now turns prospective clients away if they won't help him achieve his ultimate goal.

Braver still, he is also more selective with his existing clients. His preference is always to nurture existing clients so that they grow, and the range of services they buy grows also. But sometimes he has to, very politely, ask clients to leave because there is too much of a gap. And where that is necessary, he doesn't hesitate. Even then, however, things sometimes take a surprising turn. For example, one client he asked to leave about a year ago has recently asked to be readmitted, with an increased fee in the region of £8,000 which means that they do indeed now fit with Nick's goals for the practice!

Using Train To Gain funding innovatively

In Kent, as in many other parts of the country, Train to Gain funding means that businesses can get £1,500 of qualifying professional support for just £500 – with the other £1,000 being paid to the professional from the Train To Gain fund.

Nick realised that this means that he could earn £1,500 in fees that would only cost his clients and prospects £500. He also realised, with a smile, that the grant rules meant that he would also automatically receive every single penny of that £1,500 in advance!

So he set about designing a service that would both qualify for the grant funding and really appeal to clients and prospects.

To date 27 businesses have signed up for that service, earning him £40,500 in advance fees. Based on his experience to date, he also estimates that he will earn a further £25-30,000 in one-off additional fees from these clients as they choose to buy further services. And he has discovered that once the grant funding expires, because they have had real value from the service, most clients are willing to continue paying the full £1,500 from their own pockets. So it does tend to become a recurring fee stream.

The Calcutt Matthews Train To Gain funded service works like this:

* The practice gets an upfront payment of £1,500 – of which £500 comes from the business and £1,000 from the funding body (Update: This was how the funding worked in 2010. For 2011/12 Nick tells me that, in his area at least, clients must contribute £1000 in order to get the £1000 of funding).

- For that £1,500 fee the client gets three quarterly half day meetings (the meeting in the 4th quarter being the annual accounts meeting, which is paid for by a separate fee for the annual accounts service that they must also buy).

- In many cases those three quarterly meetings are run by a client manager, with Nick being involved only in the more complex cases.

- Where the business is "healthy and with life in it", the meetings will follow the standard One Page Plan structure used by Mayes Business Partnership (see Example of Excellence 24) and many other AVN members. In essence this means two things. Firstly, a concise quarterly report in a standard "One Page Plan" format, showing a client all the key numbers that matter in their business. (Note: This report doesn't just include the numbers that appear in a set of management accounts. It also includes other non financial numbers that the business considers to be really important). And secondly, a half day meeting to discuss the numbers in that report in a structured and systematic way.

- Where the business is "in real difficulty, perhaps even on the verge of extinction", the meetings will be specifically tailored to the urgent needs of the business. For example, in the past they have involved producing cashflow forecasts, liaising with their bank, and detailed remedial action planning.

Commenting on their success Nick said:

"Our results are good, since when you add the extra one-off fees and ongoing recurring work to the £40,500 we get in core Train To Gain fees, we will earn well over £70,000 from this initiative. But my one regret is that I wish we had started sooner – since we are only really scratching the surface, and have missed out on a lot of opportunities by being late to start. Even so, my advice to other firms is 'better late than never', so make a start now!"

Innovative strategic alliances – Part 1

Two new types of strategic alliance are paying real dividends to Calcutt Matthews.

Firstly, they now work with a number of carefully due diligenced tax planning specialists who can bring leading edge tax planning solutions to the table for Nick's clients. And there is a very clear division of labour:

- Calcutt Matthews runs seminars and have one to one discussions with clients to make them aware of their strategic alliances with third party tax specialists

- Where clients are interested, the practice will introduce them to the tax specialist

- The tax specialist does all explaining and "selling"

- Where the client wants to go ahead the tax specialist agrees a value-based fee with the client – typically 25% of the tax that will be saved

- The tax specialist enters into a separate engagement with the client, does all the technical work and bears all the engagement risk

Calcutt Matthews is rewarded for their involvement in the form of a payaway from the tax specialist:

- The payaway is fully disclosed to the client and retained under the terms of their engagement letter

- Payaways will typically be 15 to 40% of the fee paid by the client to the tax specialist

- Payaways are generally in the £2,000-£10,000 range per participating client. So across a client base the total fee potential can be very substantial indeed.

As a result, clients get the very best tax planning advice and support, and the practice earns substantial levels of additional fees in respect of that advice. As Nick explains:

"Advanced tax planning payaway income is not something I want the firm to depend on, since by its very nature it is unpredictable. But it is extremely welcome icing on the cake when it does come along, and currently local businesses do seem to have a healthy appetite for it. So the very fact that you offer advanced tax planning is a great help in winning high quality new clients."

Innovative strategic alliances – Part 2

The second innovative type of strategic alliance Calcutt Matthews have set up, is with a business coach/consultant who is able to offer advanced business advisory support to clients that is beyond the scope of an accountant's expertise.

The arrangement works as follows:

- The coach is introduced to clients as a member of the extended Calcutt Matthews team

- The coach never charges the practice a penny

- Fees earned by the coach from the practice's clients are shared – with the coach receiving 75% and Calcutt Matthews the other 25%

And it is successful because:

- Clients get advanced business advisory support that wouldn't otherwise be available to them

- The coach earns fees from those clients

- The practice adds a high quality profit centre, with no costs of any kind

- And as a result of the coach doing great work, the practice also enhances its reputation which in turns helps it to move towards its ultimate goal by winning even more quality clients

One example of how this alliance is working is the recent launch of the firm's "Business Improvement Programme" ('BIP'). They ran a seminar for 12 clients, as a result of which six have already signed up for BIP. Each of those clients pays £500, and Train to Gain Funding (see earlier) will chip in a further £1000. So the practice will receive an upfront payment of £1,500 in respect of each of the six clients – making a total of £9,000 in extra fees.

Since the BIP will be delivered by the coach – i.e. with no effort on the part of the practice – the coach will keep 75% (i.e. £6,750) and Calcutt Matthews will keep the other 25% (i.e. £2,250) as pure profit.

Explaining Nick Matthews said:

"For their £9,000 the six participating clients will meet up as a group for six half day sessions, at which they learn from the coach and from each other how to tackle the issues facing them, grow and take their businesses to the next level. I can tell you that those sessions really buzz. And I am also sure that they will also generate lots of additional work and fees for us, as clients ask us for further one-to-one help to implement the ideas generated at the BIP sessions.

What's more, NatWest have been hugely supportive, so I know that this is just the tip of the iceberg, and am very confident that this will be the first of many such BIP groups we run with our coach. After all, for us it is pretty much a no-brainer, since someone else does all the work and we earn extra fees!"

Getting a lot more referrals by giving the banks something really different

NatWest aren't the only bank helping Calcutt Mathews to grow faster than ever before. Nick and his team have uncovered a simple truth: if you are like every other accountant then you aren't giving bankers a reason to refer clients to you instead of to anybody else. So they set out to systematically give bankers a strong reason to pass clients to them.

Through their connections with AVN, the practice had co-funded the development of a comprehensive Performance Measurement and Improvement ('PMI') system that picks up where traditional accounts leave off. And by giving a copy of that system to bankers the firm has started to see a dramatic increase in the number of new referrals – winning eight high quality new clients as a direct result in the last few months alone.

Essentially the PMI system is a codification of best financial management practice. Describing how it works, Nick said:

"Everything that really matters in a business can be measured by a number. Some of the numbers that matter appear in their accounts. And some need to be measured outside the confines of their accounts. But they can all be measured as numbers using our PMI approach.

Bankers can instantly see that bringing all of those numbers together in one place, with measurement rigour and discipline, gives business owners powerful new insights into what is going on, and what they need to do to change the numbers for the better. So instead of being passive contacts, the banks we work with are actually really keen to tell their clients about us.

For the banks there are two very clear benefits: their clients are genuinely grateful for the introduction, and their clients are more likely to stay in business. While for us the benefits are even clearer...lots of high quality new clients!"

Update

The facts in the case study above are based on an interview with Nick Hume in March 2010. In March 2011 he kindly gave me this update.

"Things have continued to get better and better. Compared to three years ago our GRF is now £250,000 higher and our profits have tripled. Also the quality of our client base is better than ever before: we used to have a lot of paper bag jobs, but now we are attracting a very different kind of client. In fact, we now rarely take on a new client for less than £8,000. And in the last three months, for example, we have picked up four new clients with average fees of around £10,000 each. "

"Although we have won lots of new clients, much of our growth has come from being more proactive with existing clients – since we have found that the more proactive you are, the more they understand how else you can help them, and the more they ask you to do for them. As a result our average fees per client are now £3,700 compared to around £800 three years ago."

"Split by service line, most of our growth has come from core services.

In particular, mainstream tax planning, helping clients to understand the numbers driving their businesses, and quarterly meetings to help them create an action plan for improving their business and results."

"Another one of the keys to our success is that we are no longer cheap. We changed the way we price, using value pricing where we can (such as tax planning) and Fixed Price Agreement pricing software where we can't (such as accounts work). And, as part of this, we also increased our prices, typically by 20%, since no matter what others claim, basic maths means that you can't provide the very best service when you are cheap because there simply isn't enough time in the budget to leave no stone unturned in ensuring clients get the very best outcome."

"One of the most exciting new things we have done in the last year is to produce a short six minute video showing banks how we can help them meet their targets on our mutual clients. It is a brilliant way of grabbing their attention, and getting us to the top of the list of accountants that they refer work to. And it is an approach that is really starting to pay dividends."

"Three years ago I would have told you that all of this would be impossible to achieve, since Ashford is a really competitive market that is flooded with accountants. Yes we have lost or exited a few clients as a result of the changes. But none of the clients we wanted to keep left. And the ones that did leave were, in fact, doing us a favour since they weren't paying fair fees. Even more importantly, their departure has freed up our time to concentrate on serving our remaining clients much more proactively, and winning more of the right kind of new clients. So in a very real way, them leaving has actually helped us to grow both our top line and our bottom line."

"As a result of all this growth we are now a team of 11, and have moved into a really lovely new office with room for even more growth. In addition, my team now believes that we are the best accountants in Ashford, and it gives me great pride to agree with them."

"But actually the best thing of all for me is that I now have a much better work-life balance. Shorter working days, and genuinely not working on Friday afternoons or weekends, mean that I now have much more time for family and friends. And the key drivers of those work life balance improvements are (a) getting rid of problem clients, (b) working with a smaller number of better quality clients, (c) equipping my team with the tools, systems and training they need to do things that only I used to be able to do, and (d) properly delegating that work to the team, and rewarding them well for doing it. It is all so simple and obvious really that I kick myself for not doing it years ago!"

16 partner firm focuses on innovation

Kim Farrell is a young accountant, who in 2008 was appointed to launch new Corporate Finance and Business Advisory departments for CBHC, a 16 partner firm with offices in Chelmsford and Romford. By July 2010 his impact on the firm had been so positive that he was made a partner.

Their brochure proclaims:

"Successful businesses have financial data at their fingertips, make informed decisions based on strategic analysis and know exactly where they're going. We offer a comprehensive range of innovative financial services that will make a tangible difference to your business. Our aim is to support you to achieve your business goals.

We are passionate about your business, approach your objectives with energy and are committed to your success."

Many practices make those sorts of claims. But in my experience, in most cases they are empty promises dreamt up by a marketer with no basis in the underlying truth. At CBHC however, things are different, and the words really do reflect the reality.

Some of the things CBHC now does that set them apart are described below, and include: providing an online recruitment service, having their own television channel, helping clients hold better board meetings, as well as really focussing on getting the basics right, such as helping clients to understand what is really driving their businesses.

Graphical reports with accounts

CBHC automatically take every client's year end accounts and make them more useful by presenting them in a graphical format, with easy to understand trend analysis and benchmarking data so they can see where their strengths and weaknesses really lie.

In Kim Farrell's words: "Clients find this very, very useful, as the trends quickly show the progression of the business in a clear format. The benchmarking compares the client's business to other similar businesses in a variety of areas. By using both together, along with the financial accounts, it leads to a lot of interesting conversations with the client on future strategy and areas for improving their businesses. It is a service area that really differentiates us from our competitors, and helps us to stand out in the eyes of potential introducers. Every accountant knows this is the right thing to do, since we've been hearing it from every practice development consultant for more than twenty years. But so few firms actually take the time or trouble to do it with every client, every year. And because we are one of the few that do, we are able to command premium fees for our core services."

Attending clients' key management meetings

Board meetings are crucial to effective management, but they can lose direction and cease to have strategic value over time. So to prevent this happening to their clients, CBHC provide a BoardView service. Essentially this involves attending client's Board and other strategic meetings to help them maintain focus, not hide from difficult issues or sweep them under the carpet, and be strictly accountable for actions so that things get done rather than merely talked about. And, of course, by bringing objectivity, financial expertise and years of local and industry–wide experience to the table, their involvement also greatly aids decision making.

According to Kim Farrell, "Clients really value this service, and are happy to pay on average £300 - £500 a meeting for it. By having regular contact with clients, we can get involved in their future, and use our experience of dealing with business in a variety of sectors to offer ideas and advice. Clients often also appreciate the opportunity to speak to someone who can offer a perspective from outside their business.

So it makes a real difference to them, as well as a real difference to our fees and profitability, as each meeting generally leads to additional work. They also tell other people about it, which helps even more."

Mapping out clients' key success drivers

CBHC are passionate about helping their clients to build more successful and profitable businesses. Central to this is a commitment to using their skills with numbers to help their clients identify, map out, measure and improve the key drivers of their success. Often this includes producing a Success Driver Map for business – i.e. a simple yet mathematically precise visual representation of their business' entire sales and profit pipeline. And, once they have helped clients to understand what is really driving their businesses, they then help them use those insights to create an action plan for driving those results onwards and upwards.

Fraud consultancy service

This relatively new service is led by a fraud consultant (ex Fraud Squad) with 20 years of experience in both civil and criminal fraud. As well as the inevitable investigative and forensic support, a key part of this service involves helping victims to access litigation funding to cover the fees for solicitors, advocates and any expert testimony required to support the case. And to promote the service, they offer their clients free and confidential initial consultations to review existing security measures, and advise on how to deal with fraudulent activity if it occurs.

"Although still in its infancy this service line has the potential to generate significant fees for the practice, through supplementary work on cases, and conducting fraud audits for clients. It also adds a whole new service area for the practice, and is potentially a great source of new clients through differentiating ourselves from our competitors."

Online recruitment service

Perhaps most innovatively of all, recognising that many of their clients and contacts either want to fill a job vacancy or find someone, in late 2010 the firm launched an innovative online recruitment service, CBHC Jobs. Clients and contacts looking for a new position pay nothing to use it. While those with jobs to fill have a choice: they can either pay a fixed £250 for 28 days of online advertising, or pay a small fixed amount per completed job application they receive through the site.

The CBHC Jobs site even lets them create their own bespoke online application forms so that they capture all (and only) the information they need and weed out time wasters. It is open to any business sector, and jobs placed on it are also automatically posted to many other major job boards. And it appears to be meeting a very real need, since on the day I looked, there were 509 finance jobs in Essex and The City of London being advertised on it.

Explaining, Kim Farrell said, "This service presents us with a unique opportunity to further demonstrate the innovative services we can offer our clients. Working in conjunction with one of the UK's largest online recruiters, we are able to offer a service that can dramatically reduce our clients' recruitment costs, and aid them in getting the right candidate for their vacancies. More and more people are using the internet to search for jobs, and as the clients' accountants we can now offer them an effective recruitment solution. We are also looking to work with other accountants to give them the opportunity to have their own job boards."

Their own television channel

Well, it is not strictly a television channel, but CBHC TV does take the quality of accountant's online videos to a new level. CBHC TV is housed both in its own section on their very striking website (www.cbhc.uk.com), and also dotted context sensitively across the website.

What makes it so impressive is that each programme is professionally filmed and edited, highly informative in supporting each of the firm's main messages, and short enough for the average attention span. The videos are also kept fresh and topical – for example, at the time of writing, one of the programmes features an excellent seven minute commentary on what the recent Comprehensive Spending Review means for its clients.

"Not only is time now more valuable than ever to business leaders, but the way people take in information has changed. By having our own TV channel we can show the personality of the practice, and impart topical information quickly to clients at a time when they want. This part of our site has proved to be very popular, with some videos having in excess of 2,000 views. The videos are very cost effective to produce, particularly if you record them in blocks."

Media interest and coverage

The firm has also been extraordinarily successful in generating media coverage for its ideas and innovations, with multiple article and features about it in the Growing Business, Director and Real Business magazines, and in newspapers such as the Financial Times and The Independent.

Kim Farrell: "We see media coverage as a key part of our marketing strategy. It is important in a number of ways, particularly for giving us credibility to potential new clients and introducers, as well as helping us in our search engine rankings. Media coverage often only costs your time, and can reach far more people than advertising alone. It reinforces our message that we have experience of working with a variety of businesses and can provide opinion and comment on a number of topical issues, as well as being different to our competitors. We find we have won more engagements as a result of being quoted on sector specific issues.

There is a misconception that only large firms can provide comment and advice in the media on business issues. However in the SME sector, smaller firms have much more credibility, particularly if you can provide a real case study. The key is to act quickly, and produce press releases in real time as issues arise. To ensure that we do this we closely monitor the business press, social media and the issues that are raised by our clients. When we have identified something we can provide comment on, we contact business journalists as quickly as possible. Once you have gained some credibility with them, they will contact you for comment."

Adding value to existing compliance clients

CBHC recognised that they were attracting new clients as a result of their Business Advisory Services, but that these were usually being bought by those new clients alongside the firm's core compliance services.

So, to formalise this, and expose more of their existing compliance clients to their new approach, they have recently introduced a package of Business Advisory Services that existing and potential clients can buy, in addition to their usual compliance service. This package gives clients:

- Benchmarking reports

- Graphical accounts analysis

- A basic financial forecast

- A year-end tax health check

- Regular meetings

- A Customer Service Manager in the Business Advisory department, so that CBHC can manage the relationship and ensure good customer service and response times from other parts of the business

- A quarterly economic update, which they put together from information provided by the banks and various web sources.

- 10 free Corpfin or Fame company information reports on any company in the UK

- A free company credit rating report – since CBHC see company credit ratings being very important, and now also offer a service to help clients improve theirs, and

- The CBHC Business Club, where clients who sign up to these extra services can meet quarterly, for free, to discuss key business issues and topics that they are most interested in

Kim says: "As a base price we are charging £400 per month for this package of services, with the exact figure depending on the client. It is still early days, but in the seven weeks since its formal launch we have signed up six clients to this service, and hope to sign up 50 by the end of the year, giving us additional annual recurring income of £240k per annum."

"In addition to the £400 per month core package, clients can also buy additional services such as a more detailed financial forecast, a business plan, a One Page Plan or something else that is specific to them. We make it quite clear that these extra services are at an extra cost, and price them as a distinct project. The cost of the bundle and the extras can then be spread over 12 months, and paid by monthly direct debit."

"The feedback so far has been great and we have won pitches where we have been up against other firms sometimes much larger than us, as they are simply not offering this. The banks also value this service, as it makes their lives much easier."

What difference has all of this made to the firm?

I asked Kim what difference all of the innovations at CBHC have made to the firm and its clients over the last couple of years, and he said this:

"The feedback from clients, contacts and referral sources has been phenomenal, as demonstrated by the growth in the Business Advisory department which had a turnover of £120,000 in year one, and £300,000 in year two. We are on course for a turnover of £480,000 in year three.

There is a real buzz around us in the business community, and we have enjoyed consistently increasing levels of enquiries and referrals. We also know that our new services have played an important role in helping our clients to survive and even grow in a tough market.

We have of course lost some clients, but have replaced them with more profitable customers as a result of our approach. The average spend per client has also increased – for example, a client that has traditionally spent £2,500 every year for a long time, spent £30,000 with us in 2009. This is not uncommon."

Success comes by helping clients to achieve their goals

Clear Vision is a two director practice with 12 team members. Based on the high street of the quiet Wiltshire market town of Corsham, eight miles from Bath, they certainly don't have any obvious geographical advantage. And yet what they have achieved is something that, in my experience, most accountants all too readily dismiss with pre-judgements such as "that won't work" or "things are different around here."

Their current results are stunning:

- Turnover is in excess of £700,000.

- And with only approximately 130 business clients and 20 tax return only clients, their average fees are in excess of £5,000.

- In the last year they won £160,000 of new clients.

- The 46 year old Managing Director Rob Walsh works an average of 40 hours a week, takes 14 weeks holiday a year, and in each of the last five years has taken home profits of between £200,000 and £280,000.

It all starts with values

Explaining how it all started, the firm's founder Rob Walsh said, "I did not want to call my business Rob Walsh Accountancy, so I chose a name that summed up perfectly what the practice is about. To me the most important thing an accountant can do is help a client identify and articulate what they really want out of their business and their life, and then help them to achieve it. That's the way we really make a difference. Ultimately it is about being in partnership with your clients, and not merely having a transactional sales ledger / purchase ledger relationship with them."

He also said, "It all starts with your core values. Our core values are to build proper relationships with a manageable number of clients so we really can help them to achieve their goals. And also to deliver our services in an open, honest and straightforward way, to a very high quality, at the speed the client wants us to go at, and always focused on giving advice and support that they really value."

When they come from Rob, these words are certainly not clichés or glib marketing speak. They come from the heart, are the bedrock of the

Clear Vision culture, and as you will see, are evidenced in everything the firm actually does.

Focussing on your clients' goals

The day I interviewed Rob for this book he had just spent the morning emailing a large chunk of his client base to ask them about their specific goals for 2011. And this is something clients have come to expect, since right at the very start of every client relationship the Clear Vision team uses a systematic approach to:

- Help the client to identify their business and personal goals – and to articulate them in precise detail in writing

- Understand what the end game is for the client – i.e. what they want the business to look like when it is done, and when and how they want to exit

- Evaluate whether Clear Vision can make a significant contribution towards helping the client achieve all of that

According to Rob:

"Most accountants don't seem to realise how much they can do to help their clients achieve their goals. The reality is that by helping clients to make their businesses work better, earn more and keep more of what they earn, you can make a huge contribution.

For example, if you help someone make their business work better, so there are fewer problems, less hassle, and a shorter working week you are literally helping them to get their life back, spend more time with their family, and have more time for their other passions and interests.

And if you help someone make their business more financially successful, you are giving them the means to pay for the things they have dreamed of (fast cars, holiday homes, exotic holidays, early retirement etc), or to pay for starter homes for their children, better nursing care for their elderly parents, or even the much needed funds for the good causes they care deeply about. When you really think about it, the difference a good accountant can make is profound."

Ideal clients

If Clear Vision feels that they can't make a significant contribution towards helping someone achieve their goals, they won't accept them as a client. In fact, there are three criteria that someone has to meet in order to be accepted as a client:

1. They must like them – since life is too short to waste working with people you don't like

2. They must be able to help them achieve their goals – since that is one of the firm's core values, and

3. They must be able to create a "story" out of their relationship – the significance of which is explained in the next section

Marketing stories

As I interviewed Rob he constantly backed up what he was saying by quoting the firm's key performance indicators – a feat I later discovered was made possible by his use of a One Page Plan to capture and share all the key numbers with his entire team.

One of the most impressive numbers was the £160,000 of new clients they had won in the last 12 months. He was even able to instantly tell me that £5,000 of this came from the firm's striking website (www.clearvisionaccountancygroup.co.uk), £17,000 from walk-ins, £70,000 from client referrals and £68,000 from seminars, events and other speaking engagements.

Every accountant knows that referrals are the best way to grow a practice. So instead of passively waiting for referrals, Rob has developed systems to actively encourage them. At the heart of these systems is the idea of telling 'stories' – i.e. true 'in their own words' accounts of how Clear Vision has helped people to achieve their goals. These stories are presented in various formats, including written case studies, testimonial letters, and high quality videos on their website. Most powerfully of all, they are also delivered in person, as clients regularly agree to join Rob on stage when he is speaking to explain the difference Clear Vision has made to their lives. Therefore, much of the £68,000 from events and speaking is also largely down to the power of word of mouth advertising.

According to Rob:

"Every practice should have a library of really strong stories it can call on whenever it needs them since they are the most powerful form of marketing imaginable. And any practice that can't pull together that sort of library needs to take a long hard look at why it isn't making enough of a difference to its clients.

The bottom line is this: clients are much more likely to believe another client when they say you are good, than if you said it yourself. So the key to effective marketing is to give clients great service in a way that makes a real difference to them, and then turn that into a marketing story that can be told over and over again. That is how you make the very most of word of mouth."

The Clear Vision Club

One of the systems they use to make the most of these stories is The Clear Vision Club. Two or three times a year Rob teams up with a leading IFA. Each invites four of their respective clients to join them for dinner. The seating plan for dinner involves a circular table for 10, with Rob's clients sitting at every other seat so that they have a non client on both sides of them.

Everyone is then asked to explain their goals to the people sitting next to them. And what then automatically happens is that Rob's clients start telling the story of how Clear Vision has helped them to achieve their goals, and the non clients in the room get very excited about asking Clear Vision to do the same for them. It is a simple yet incredibly powerful system that works really well.

Dental specialisation

Seven years ago the practice only had two dentists as clients. Today almost 50% of its fees come from the dental profession. And because they have developed a national reputation, only 25% of their dental clients are within a 25 mile radius of Corsham, and the rest are spread across the country, proving that good clients are more interested in what you can do for them than in where you are based.

"For the last few years all of our marketing efforts and budget has been directed at the dentists, and it has really paid off. Not only have we won dental clients across the UK, but happy dentists have given us lots of referrals to their non dentist contacts. So our core business has benefited too."

There is a separate identity, marketing message and website (www.clearvisiondental.co.uk) for this side of the business. They regularly speak at seminars and conferences for dentists, and invite a lot of dentists to the Clear Vision Club. They also capture the contact details of prospective clients by offering a free report called "The 12 most powerful insights every dentist needs to know to transform the results of their practice."

In 2011 they will be publishing their first book: a 33,000 word volume called "The Business of Dentistry – How You Run a Successful and Profitable Dentistry Practice." And, having seen the manuscript, I can tell you it is extremely good, and will be an extremely powerful marketing tool for the firm.

Pricing strategy

Everything the practice does is centred on what its clients want, including the way they price. So they agree a fixed price in advance for every single piece of work, and also give every client what they describe as a "big hairy guarantee."

The guarantee is spelled out like this on their website: "You know how bad it makes you feel when someone doesn't live up to your expectations? We're confident that you will feel our services are worth every penny. But if ever you feel the value you receive does not exceed the price you pay, you can – literally – pay the amount you feel is appropriate. It's our guarantee to you." Explaining their pricing strategy Rob Walsh says:

"Time based billing has the bizarre potential of rewarding accountants for being slow, and is the exact opposite of what clients really want. So we always agree a fixed price and prepare a fixed price agreement upfront before any work begins. Clients love it because they know precisely how much they will be charged and never receive a surprise bill.

They also love the guarantee, because it means they know they will always end up paying a price that they feel is fair. And because of our commitment to providing great service in a way that makes a real difference, we never have to lose sleep about there being a big hole in our P&L account because of clients triggering the guarantee. In fact we have been paid for all of the fixed fees we have issued and have never had to give a refund under the guarantee. So, far from costing us money, when you take into account that it helps many more people to make the decision to work with us, the guarantee actually makes us money.

The other key aspect to our pricing strategy is that we are categorically not cheap, and we never compete on price. We don't have to, since by focussing on the things that really matter to clients – i.e. helping them to achieve their goals – and guaranteeing our work, they are happy to pay premium prices. In fact, if we were cheap it would be counter-productive, since there wouldn't be enough in the kitty to provide a genuinely first class service without making compromises somewhere along the line."

Importantly, Clear Vision's fixed fees are fully inclusive of unlimited access to their team for advice on ad-hoc matters. "This means clients feel free to pick up the phone to speak to us whenever they need to," explains Rob, "and that is exactly what we want them to do, since the more problems they bring to us the more solutions we can provide and that in turn means the more fees we earn."

A pricing approach that works for clients

Clients seem to love the firm's approach to pricing. For example, on their website there is a video in which client Robert Craven (the internationally published business author and renowned business guru who founded the Directors' Centre) tells his story of working with Clear Vision, saying:

"One of the things that was grinding me down with previous accountants was this insistence on charging by the hour, and to my mind that meant they had no reason to work more quickly. Clear Vision have turned all of that upside down, which is an absolute win for me. Because I have a fixed price agreement I can phone them whenever I need, they always do things for me as quickly as possible and they always give me an absolute commitment on turnaround times. They also get me to make monthly payments throughout the year so I don't get a big bill at the end of the year."

(Note: To make it work on the page the above slightly condenses and paraphrases what Robert Craven says on the video, but when you watch it you will see that I have stayed entirely true to his message).

Getting the best from the team

In addition to their regular team, Clear Vision also has two independent non executives who attend its quarterly Board meetings. One is a nationally respected marketing specialist, and the other a retired (but still young) managing partner from a much larger and very innovative accountancy practice. "Having non executives of their calibre isn't cheap, but you have to invest in quality, and they have made a vital contribution to our success," says Rob. "They make sure we see the wood from the trees, challenge our assumptions, ask the difficult questions we would sometimes prefer to brush under the carpet, and ensure we don't fall into the trap of sloppy thinking. That kind of input is priceless."

A key element of the culture and core values of the practice is openness and honesty. So all the key numbers of the business are shared with the entire team in the form of a monthly One Page Plan. "This shows our team we trust them, creates a sense of ownership, and both motivates and enables them to take the actions needed to continually make things better."

"We don't just leave our team to sink or swim," explains Rob. "We have developed systems to guide and support them at every turn. In fact System Builder, the software tool that manages our systems, is the brain of our business. Our systems have taken a long time to develop, test and fine tune, but they are central to our success because they allow us to do everything to the same best practice standard every time. So we never waste time reinventing the wheel, or doing things sub-optimally. And because of their power, we now literally have systems for everything, from how we do technical work to what we do to wow our clients. As a result our team is able to work quickly and to the very highest standards, which drives up quality at the same time as driving down delivery times and costs."

Clear Vision also publicly acknowledges, celebrates and rewards the outstanding contribution of its team members in several innovative ways. For example, they have a quarterly award for the team member that gives the most ideas or wows in that quarter, and also an annual award for the team member of the year. The latter is voted for anonymously by every team member, every month, and at the end of the year the person with the most votes wins an all expenses paid, four day trip for two to New York, Paris or Monaco. As Rob says "These awards involve us putting our money where our mouth is, and showing that we really do value what our people do. They also motivate us all to raise our game and really go the extra mile for clients. And they help us all to feel really proud about the things we do for each other and for our clients."

Wowing clients

Wowing clients is something that the entire Clear Vision team is passionate about. For example, when my colleagues and I have visited their offices over the years (and they assure me that we did not get special treatment) we were wowed in many ways, including:

- A red carpet being rolled out for us between the car park and front door (I kid you not!)

- A library of carefully chosen leading edge business books for clients to borrow

- Asking me what my favourite song is and then playing it on the genuine Wurlitzer juke box in the area we chatted prior to our meetings, and

- Remembering to play the same song the next time I visited

- Instead of displaying standard pictures, their walls feature a combination of amusing caricatures of the team and large prints of stunning photographs taken by Rob on his holidays (not family snaps, of course, but the occasional really good landscape and cityscape photos that we all take from time to time)

- Being challenged to a space hopper race (apparently they are selective about who they offer this to!) that brought lots of happy childhood memories flooding back to me

- A bowl of fresh fruit and mints on every meeting room table

- A choice of different teas and coffees served in exquisite bone china cups and saucers

- And on leaving, discovering that our car had been valeted and that there was a little box on the dashboard containing some coins and a note explaining that they were exactly the change we would need for the toll bridge we had to cross on our onwards journey into Wales. Talk about attention to detail!

The reaction of clients

But Clear Vision doesn't just excel at the above sort of "sexy" experiential stuff that makes interacting with them enjoyable and memorable. They are also obsessive about the fundamentals of customer care, and measure every aspect of their performance.

For example, knowing how important speed is to clients, they measure turnaround times, and in 2010 achieved an average accounts turnaround time of 18 days. And because openness and honesty are core values, they also publish their performance metrics (warts and all) prominently on their website and on the wall where every visitor to their office can see it.

Those metrics show that clients really appreciate the Clear Vision way of doing things. For example, according to business guru Frederick Reicheld, the only question any business needs to ask its customers is how likely they are to recommend the business to others. So Clear Vision measures that in their annual client delight survey (and notice the word 'delight', because according to Rob Walsh "it is not enough to satisfy clients, you have to go much further and delight them").

And in their 2010 survey, on a scale of 1-10, their clients gave the firm a resounding thumbs up with score of 9.48.

Why are their clients so happy? The answer can probably be found when you watch the video on their website of Robert Craven explaining the impact the practice has had on him and his business (and this time these are verbatim quotes): "I know that Clear Vision has made us more profitable. I know that Clear Vision has helped us to increase our turnover. And I know that Clear Vision has helped us to run a better business."

Any practice that delivers those sorts of results is bound to have very happy clients, who are happy to pay big fees, isn't it?

The challenge to the profession

Having experienced in Clear Vision what a really good accountant can do for his business, Robert Craven ends his video interview by saying: "If you are not delighted and ecstatically happy with your accountant, and you don't think your accountant is helping you to get more customers, get more sales, get more profits, get more cash into your business then you should change accountant. It's as simple as that."

That message could be a ticking time bomb for many practices, and a huge opportunity for others who follow in Clear Vision's footsteps. If their clients start to hear and respond to it, some practices will start haemorrhaging fees and profits, while others will grow exponentially.

Sole practitioner who no longer feels the need to do everything personally

This Bodmin-based practice was established seventeen years ago and has dealt mainly with compliance work. However, Principal Paul Miller felt he was becoming "chained to the desk" and needed to change the business. The outcome was a major restructuring of the organisation and a markedly different firm at the end of it.

Identifying the shortcomings

According to Paul, twelve months ago the practice faced a number of jugular problems and failings, including:

- There was little team buy-in or ethos.

- No real operational structure was in place.

- Too many bad debts were incurred (£39,000 in the previous two years).

- There were a lot of small clients who paid annual fees of less than £400.

- The principal was working in the business rather than on it, dealing with a minimum of four appointments per day and 15-20 phone calls per day. He also prepared the majority of the tax returns.

- There was an inability to set a clear vision and a tendency to latch on to any idea or book that would help. "In all honesty," comments Paul, "we were always searching for the answer but never finding it."

It was clear that something needed to be done if the practice was to move forward.

Creating time for planning and action

In order to make the necessary changes, the first task was to ensure that Paul had the available time to focus on it. So, in the first instance, he delegated every single tax return to team members in order create some slack in his working week to work on improving the business.

And to make sure that really happened, he also blocked out time in his diary one afternoon a week, specifically for working "on" the business. During this time, all incoming calls and emails are blocked so there are no distractions.

As a result he was able to put a number of critical measures in place, including:

- A plan was created to specifically target the preferred work that Paul wanted the firm to be doing a lot more of. Higher value work that is more enjoyable for the team and generates significantly higher fees for the firm.

- Sharing the vision and goals with the team resulting in team buy-in.

- An efficient team structure was devised, with clear roles and responsibilities, and step by step systems were created to make it easier for people to fulfil their roles.

- Team members of the right calibre were recruited using psychometric testing to understand their motivation and soft skills.

- Key Performance Indicators were identified and tested, with forecasts then measured against actual values.

"There is still a long way to go", says Paul, "but already the benefits to me personally are immense. I have a better work life balance, am enjoying the work more and banking more money."

Focusing on ideal clients

Having decided on the type of work they really wanted to do, the next step was to rationalise the client base in order to generate more of that kind of work. This involved a number of steps:

- Identifying an ideal client profile and implementing a minimum fee policy of £1,500.

- Making a policy decision not to take on any new audit work.

- Managing away many of the bottom quartile clients. "This was emotionally difficult," says Paul, "as many had been clients for over ten years." Nevertheless, the process continues, as Paul confirms: "Over the last month, we have exited the 15% of our clients who were paying us the lowest fees, with no overall reduction in our fee income."

- Replacing the bottom quartile with higher fees based on a three, four and five star pricing model, and using top down pricing to show them the most expensive options first.

- Exiting the difficult clients (slow payers, poor record keeping, uncommunicative) by referring them to another practice.

- Instead of having an all-comers policy, two out of three prospects that approach the practice are now turned away based on the minimum fee policy of £1,500. Instead, they are referred to another practice in return for 40% of the first year's income that they earn from the client and £40 for every tax return-only enquiry that is passed to them.

"The main benefit of passing on leads and clients to another practice," remarks Paul, "has not been the money, welcome as it is, but the freeing up of capacity to serve other clients more proactively and to have quality thinking time."

He adds: "Our general pricing philosophy now is the same as exclusive country clubs – i.e. that it is highly desirable to be a client and therefore you must pay for the privilege."

Improving fee income

Rationalising the client base also gave the opportunity to change the fee structure, since the remaining clients were better able to justify higher fees. This restructuring was approached on a number of fronts:

- Reviewing the fee levels with the help of the Times Up pricing software. Paul gives an example: "We took on a client at 350% of what we would have previously charged. At our original fee level we would have lost money. But now it is one of our largest fees."

- Charging higher fees for incorporations and other tax planning work based on the value of the tax savings made. "This has allowed us to do a much better job for clients, and in some cases has also helped us to earn 700% more than we would have done under our old approach."

- Identifying under recoveries on existing clients and either eliminating them by increasing fees, or passing the client to another accountant for an introducer's fee.

- Offering additional services, such as benchmarking and management accounts, which has helped to increase the average fee per client by 28% over the last three years. In fact, adds Paul, "The biggest increase as a direct result of the changes has been 75% for one non audit client."

Looking after clients' entire life cycle

Croucher Needham is a four-partner practice with an exciting vision, supported by a powerful model, for addressing each of the main stages of the business life cycle.

The aim, according to Director Malcolm Kauder, is for Croucher Needham not to be simply considered as 'an accountancy practice'. To achieve this aim, the firm, which has offices in London, Bedford and Saffron Walden, has taken a close look at how it meets the needs of its clients and communicates its approach to its clients.

The outcome is the "Croucher Needham Success Model" that covers the four stages of a company's business life cycle. The thinking behind this is that the practice can take on a client at any point in its development and help it through the remaining stages.

"The Directors and team have a very clear marketing message now" explains Malcolm. "With a strong focused structure and framework, everyone in Croucher Needham should become confident to explain how we can assist entrepreneurs and quickly make clear to them how we can help. They can provide examples of the tools that we have available and can confidently explain the benefits they will obtain."

"When the programme is explained, clients can quickly see that as a firm, we truly are a little bit different and have a clear structured approach to the way we can deliver services. If we take 'start up' businesses, for example, they can work through the whole programme with us, feeling confident that their future success isn't simply a result of haphazard and lucky decisions."

Developing a capital growth approach

All clients aren't suitable for the programme and so, as Malcolm explains, the challenge is to select the ones that are: "We quickly identify clients that have no aspiration to go beyond earning a good living and those that are actually open to develop a capital growth approach. For those in the latter category, we can apply the strength of our model so that they can work through the programme with us. We help to open the minds of those business owners that haven't really thought about it that much and we can look to mentor them in the future."

The approach, which has been trademarked, is called "Emerge, Grow, Realise and Protect", which neatly summarises the four main stages of the business life cycle:

- **Emerging** businesses with new ideas and ventures
- **Growing** and developing the business
- **Realising** the vision
- **Protecting** what has been created.

This model allows Croucher Needham to focus on key areas for each client, rather than trying to put across a large number of services that are often not relevant. It also means staff can be trained on specific subjects and so become experts in particular fields rather than undertaking general work. This gives them enhanced career prospects by them gaining knowledge and expertise in the core areas in which they are involved.

Planning for growth

The new programme is at a relatively early stage of rollout but, according to Malcolm "there has been tremendous feedback from prospects and referrers." As a result, there is huge confidence in its future.

Malcolm also says: "Our commercial model using the approach is not to only grow organically. We have a strong, conscious strategy to go out into the market and to provide solutions and options for the 'baby boomer' practices that currently have no succession in place and so will be looking to retire.

As experienced, ambitious partners, we are looking to continue to grow by aggressive acquisition year on year. As we bring on such new clients, we can introduce them to our model and show how we can add value. We can then identify where clients might actually sit within it, so that we can offer and serve them in the appropriate way, having understood their needs. With this, we believe we stand a good chance of retaining clients going forward. This commercially helps the exiting partners to maximise their earn-outs and so, with this in mind, we hope to be able to attract ongoing subsequent acquisition targets."

Whilst rolling out its new programme, Croucher Needham continues to look further ahead, as Malcolm confirms: "As an example of future developments and in order to support the Emerge part of the model, we are currently being introduced to the London Business School. We hope to become mentors to early stage businesses and are looking to invest our time and energy in nurturing entrepreneurial talent.

We are also in the process of building our own international network, already having strong relationships in most of Asia, parts of Europe and South America. Once these relationships are cemented more formally, we can start to introduce our partners' solutions to our own model. As an example, we will be able provide overseas asset protection."

Tax credits change a sole practitioner's life

David Scott is a sole practitioner from Newton Aycliffe in County Durham who works with a team of two – his wife and daughter.

"There are three important dates you need to know about me" he says. "1948 when I was born. 1972 when I qualified. And 20 July 2010 when I went on a tax credits course that changed my life."

How tax credits have transformed the firm's profitability

Prior to the course the practice was serving a lot of small clients and had annual fees of £110,000. But as a result of starting to offer his clients a tax credits service, in the next six months David earned a further £45,000 in fees. And since all those extra fees were generated by his existing team from the existing client base, there were no marketing costs and almost every penny flowed through to his bottom line.

"Traditionally, like so many other firms, we had kept well away from tax credits" explained David. "But on the course I realised two things. Firstly, that there was a huge commercial opportunity. And secondly, that there was a clue in the title: the word 'tax' in tax credits meant they were part of the tax system, and therefore as professionals we owed it to our clients to get involved."

Being proactive around tax credits

He continued: "The most over-used word in the profession is 'proactive'. We all use it, and we all hope it impresses clients. In this context, what proactivity does not mean is circulating all clients proudly announcing that 'we now have a Tax Credit service'. Most clients will simply ignore such an announcement. Either because they do not know what a 'Tax Credit service' is. Or because, mistakenly in many cases, they think it does not apply to them."

"What proactivity does mean is reviewing all clients, and categorising their tax credits entitlement as 'definite', 'possible' or 'probably not' (for example, because their income levels are far too high)."

"And then you need to contact each of the 'definite' and 'possible' clients in turn, telling them that they may be entitled to tax credits, or to more tax credits, and arrange a meeting to explore the opportunities. That is exactly what we did, and I can tell you it works phenomenally well."

In fact, David was so excited at the prospect that the day after the course he was at his desk by 7am, and by 9am had data-mined and categorised every single one of his clients.

The two main types of tax credit opportunities

David found that there were two main types of tax credit opportunities with his clients:

- Those that are not claiming at all – usually because either, they didn't realise they could, or because falling income during the recession meant that they have only recently become eligible

- And those that are not claiming as much as they could

Many clients who fall into the first category are confused by the title "Working Families Tax Credits" and simply did not realise that you do not have to have a family to make a claim.

Clients however are generally in the latter category for two reasons. Either because, like accountants, they find the process complicated and so don't get their claims right. Or because they are completely unaware of the many legitimate tax credit planning strategies that can be used to increase the amounts they are entitled to.

"As I see it" says David, "all of these factors mean that accountants have a moral and professional duty to ensure that their clients don't miss out on what is rightfully theirs."

How tax credits can change clients' lives

The new service is having a big effect on David's clients. For example, one client was ecstatic when David helped him increase his entitlement from £6,000 to just over £8,000 because it meant his wife could afford to give up work to look after their new baby.

And with the very first client David approached, he was able to help them to increase their entitlement from £185 to £810 a month. "When I rang to tell them the news they literally whooped and cheered with joy."

It is also helping him to win new clients: "A business contact came in to talk about referrals, and started to moan in a jokey way about his kids. So as a throwaway comment I said 'well, at least the four kids are worth £14,300 a year to you in tax credits'. That stopped him in his tracks, because his accountant hadn't ever suggested he should claim. So I showed him how we could help and he became a client there and then. And I am sure there are many more new clients out there just like that for me too."

Making it work commercially

"The very first claim I did took me almost two days" says David. "But now we could probably do it in less than half an hour. That's because we have now got to grips with the technical issues by making the most of our compliance software from the Tax Credits Team. Obviously there was a learning curve, but it is all much easier than I used to think it would be."

As for pricing, David charges £195 for a single person, or £295 for a couple for filling in a tax credit return, plus a one off fee of 25% of the extra tax credits he helps clients to get. "The very first client I explained our prices to, tried to negotiate me down to 20%, but I stood firm. And that is pretty much the only issue I've had with price. As far as clients are concerned, I am helping them to get extra cash, so they are delighted."

Further benefits

David says that the benefits go far beyond the very substantial extra fees he is earning. "We have very impressed and very happy clients, and are getting a lot more referrals."

"And there is also one further payback that I had not anticipated" he added. "As 30% of my clients are now in the tax credits system, and they need the Annual Declaration completing by 31 July, by encouraging them to provide the final figures, rather than provisional figures, we will also be able to complete their self assessment tax returns using much the same figures. And that is a lot of tax returns we won't have to do in January next year!"

The new regime

According to David: "It is no longer good enough for accountants to hide behind the excuse that 'tax credits are hard'. Everything we do is hard. That's why clients need us and why they are willing to pay us. In fact, it is the very reason we exist."

"It is also not good enough to hide behind the excuse that 'tax credits are changing, so we won't get involved'. Change is a given in so many areas of our work, especially tax. And we always have to do the best job for clients before and after each and every change."

"There are still many ways to help clients under the tax credit systems as it stands today. So that is exactly what we should be doing: helping them today. And with luck there will also be many things we can do to help them after it all changes too."

What to do when your partners want proof that change is a good idea

Ian Williams is a partner in a traditional four partner practice in rural west Wales. In 2008 he felt that the firm needed to broaden its service offering, but his partners were not convinced of the need or the likely benefits.

In many partnerships that would probably have been the end of the matter. But to their credit, the four partners here took a much more mature approach, and agreed that Ian could set up a separate business to pilot the idea, provided that he didn't ask them to invest any time or money in it.

So Elite Tax and Business Solutions LLP was launched as a new partnership between Ian, members of his family, and an IFA.

A runaway success

"On one level the new business is very small, since it has no full time employees, very few overheads and runs out of the same offices as the practice," explains Ian.

"But on another level it has been a runaway success. In the first 18 months our turnover was £176,000, and it has generated almost the same level of profits for me as I was earning from the compliance practice. So in effect I have nearly doubled my personal income. And I know from what is already in the pipeline, that there is much more still to come."

"To put these results into context, you need to understand that rural Wales is a hard market, and Fishguard where we are based is a small market town with a population of only 6,000 people. So we don't have all the advantages of a prosperous larger town or city. But even here there is plenty of demand for advanced tax planning services."

The two keys to this success

The first key to the new venture's success is its delivery mechanism. "If we had tried to build an advanced tax planning team from scratch it would have taken a lot of time, and cost a lot of money. So that wasn't an option," says Ian.

"Instead we have linked up with a panel of the UK's best tax planning specialists, and they do the work to an incredibly high standard without it costing us a penny. They do the technical work (which is usually so advanced that no small or medium sized practice could have done it in-house anyway), they take the engagement risk, and they invoice the client. For our part, we charge the tax specialist a fee, or 'payaway', for supporting them, and we also usually charge our clients a fee for helping them to implement the advice they receive from the tax specialist."

The second key to their success has been that they have focused on the 450 or so current clients of Ian's existing practice.

"The easiest way to hit the ground running was to offer the new tax planning services to our existing clients. Once we started systematically showing our clients how much they could save, they got really excited. I also get the same reaction when I meet prospects for the compliance practice too, so it really helps me to convert them into clients. The other key benefit is that it is helping us to get a lot more referrals, as excited clients tend to tell other people, and that has a powerful snowball effect."

"Overall I get a positive response from about 90% of the people I talk to, although you can never tell who will and won't be interested. It is therefore vital to tell everyone, since if you prejudge whether they will be interested you will often be wrong, and will be letting down the clients you don't tell."

"Given that the business specialises in advanced tax planning, we are also able to use Penn Report planning and the fact that we are an LLP to obtain some very dramatic tax savings for ourselves. In fact, we estimate that they will be equivalent to our first five years of profits being effectively tax free, which really helps too."

The four morals

Ian believes that there are four morals to his story:

1. **Clients want lower tax bills** – "Even in rural Wales the appetite for advanced tax planning is phenomenal. And if that is what clients want, that is what we should be doing."

2. **Make tax planning easy** – "By forming strategic alliances with specialists who will share their fees with you, you get the best of all worlds: first class solutions and service for your clients, highly profitable income for the practice, and all with less effort and engagement risk than if you did the work yourself."

3. **Don't let your partners get in the way** – "If you really want to do something, but your partners aren't yet convinced, find a mutually agreeable way of giving it a go within your sphere of influence. After all, it is your life, and it is not right for other people's agendas, beliefs and prejudices to stop you living it to the full."

4. **It is not about being superman** – "I would describe myself as ordinary and of average ability. For example, I got a third class honours degree, and scraped through my professional exams. But I am passionate about doing the right things for clients, and that is what really counts. So if I can do it, anyone can."

Helping to build businesses

The two partners at Aberdeen-based Fyfe Moir were already earning six-figure profits, so their desire to do something different wasn't driven by a need for additional financial gain. Instead, as partner Graham Fyfe points out, there was a more altruistic motive: "What we saw was an opportunity to create more enjoyable work and to really make a difference with the services we provide."

Running a seminar on "Pricing for maximum profit "

"We are great believers of going after the low hanging fruit first, doing the things we find we can develop easily and profit from first, and leaving the difficult stuff until later," says Graham. "Of course, what we find easy may be difficult for others and vice versa."

Inspired by 2020, and supported by the Harris Walter's Strategic Planning Toolkit, co-partner Alan Moir had already done a lot of business consulting work in the past, and really enjoyed it. So on joining AVN in 2010, Fyfe Moir decided to build on this by launching a 'Business Builder Forum' using the ready to use seminars their membership gave them.

Initially they dipped their toe in the water by running a standalone seminar on 'Pricing for maximum profit' that they thought would be an ideal subject to introduce the service to the practice's client base, prospects and contacts. Of course, the quandary for any new venture is what to charge. They decided to go for £50 plus VAT per attendee, which they considered a justifiable fee for such a powerful seminar.

A total of thirty invitations were sent out for an early morning event and an excellent response resulted in twenty attendees and £1,000 in ticket sales. "The presentation went down very well and the feedback from all attendees was very positive," comments Graham.

Turning it into an ongoing business club

The initial seminar was so successful in fact, that they decided to turn it into a regular Business Builder Forum club that would run throughout 2011. Places were offered for an annual membership fee of £600 plus VAT, which covers ten meetings a year lasting two hours each.

The first hour of every meeting is a presentation by Fyfe Moir on a high impact business topic. And the second hour is a free-form session at which delegates both discuss the issues raised in the formal presentation and share their own ideas and insights to help each other tackle their challenges and become more successful.

Substantial direct and indirect benefits

A short time later the club had already attracted 17 members. "So far, we have run two of the ten 2011 meetings and feedback remains very positive," remarks Graham. "We also have a small waiting list for a further group to run on Mondays, and are looking to roll it out by June 2011. Membership fees are already worth £10,200 a year to us, and we expect this to increase."

There are many other spin-off benefits too, as Graham explains: "It is also helping us to win new clients. For example, we have already converted one Business Builder Forum member into a compliance client with recurring annual fee income of £4,800. That client had been with the same accountancy firm for 32 years, but what they saw from us at the Business Builder Forum, and the benchmarking we do, was enough to convince them to work with us instead."

"Of course, it is not all about money. Our team is getting exposure to new business skills and concepts. And, for my partner Alan in particular, being paid to develop business is a great thrill. So it is giving a further boost to our already massive enthusiasm for the job in hand."

In addition, the profile of Fyfe Moir has been enhanced as its PR provider has been able to use the Business Builder Forum to promote the practice through the local press. "Our reputation is also being enhanced by club members, most of whom are 'raving fans' and talk about us a lot," adds Graham.

A word of warning

However, for any firms that are planning to change or extend their range of services, Graham advises caution: "We believe firms should remember what got them where they are currently and not try to change everything at once. Instead you should focus on something you truly believe will benefit all three stakeholders: i.e. you, your team and your clients."

"From there, build up on the services offered, adding one layer at a time. Certainly don't 'throw the baby out with the bathwater'. Test everything and continue with that which works, consigning the rest to the waste paper basket, or to a time in the future when you can do it justice."

Spectacular revenue gains

This one partner practice, with offices in Central London, Wimbledon, Croydon and Clapham, has put a lot of effort into making more services available for its clients and into providing those services more efficiently.

As a result it has achieved some spectacular results, as practice principal Gordon D'Silva explains: "Over the last couple of years we have doubled our fees, reduced our costs per client by 22%, trebled our profits and have happier clients than ever before."

New services that make a real difference

Gordons Knight hasn't just tinkered with its services by making minor improvements and offering marginal extras. Instead, it has focused on providing heavyweight services that make a real difference to its clients. Some of its main innovations include:

1. **The Entrepreneurs' Club** is a profit building service that has been actively promoted to clients. The service costs £500 per month and provides each client with a monthly meeting that lasts 2-3 hours and aims to help them make significant increases in their profits. Gordon says, "It is still early days, but we have already had six clients take us up on it."

   Although most clients like the idea of the club, some are reluctant or unable to pay the monthly fee. For these clients, a 'no win, no fee' version is available. In these cases, the client agrees to pay a fixed percentage of any increase in profit that results from the help and advice that is provided. "They love it," comments Gordon D'Silva. "The profits of participating companies have risen rapidly and, as a result, we have been paid handsomely for our time. Of course each client has benefitted at least four times more."

   For example, a web development company that took up the no win, no fee deal saw its income quadruple within six months. A member of the company enthused: "The no win, no fee option that Gordons Knight offers is a no brainer. You have nothing to lose and everything to gain. Using simple business principles and low cost alternatives, Gordon has changed how we think about our business, pricing and profitability."

2. **Advanced tax planning** had not traditionally been a strength for Gordons Knight. It remedied this by using the contacts of a respected accountancy network to tap into a panel of leading tax boutiques that it is now proud to work in partnership with, to bring leading edge tax solutions to the

benefit of its clients. Gordon remarks: "Where we had nothing to offer, we can now compete with the biggest firms by helping clients save thousands of pounds in tax. For example, one client bought six investment properties at a 20% discount with the tax money he saved by using the advanced tax strategies we introduced him to. In the past we had no tax specialism; in fact, we hated tax. Now we love the ideas we get from the tax providers. And our clients love the savings we are able to help them obtain."

3.   **Credit checking reports** are provided free of charge to clients. These are available through the practice's membership of a leading credit profile provider, which allows virtually unlimited searches and risk profiles. Clients also get a free credit control advisory pack containing detailed suggestions on how they can improve their cash flow. "In these tough times, the benefits to clients cannot be overstated," says Gordon.

4.   **Free Accounts Software** ('Gordons Knight Online') is offered to clients using an application that is licensed and 'white labelled' from an online accounts software provider. This software helps those clients maintain better books and records as well as managing their profitability and cash flow in a more effective manner. For example, one innovative way it does this is by emailing the client when a sales invoice becomes overdue for payment, thereby helping the client to reduce the incidence and extent of late payments and avoid bad debts. According to Gordon, "Clients really like the fact that we give them this software for free. And we benefit because not only does the software make it easier for us to produce their accounts, but it also helps us give more accurate business benefitting advice regularly to clients." (NB: If you want Gordon to tell you which software he uses for this he has asked me to invite you to contact him on gds@gordonsknight.co.uk).

Higher fees and guaranteed savings

As a consequence of these improvements, the fees Gordons Knight charges to new clients have been increased by around 25% to cover the systems, procedures and pro-activity measures offered as standard to their clients. Unsurprisingly therefore, some prospective clients ask why the firm's fees are often some 30% higher than those charged by comparable competition.

In these cases, the usual response is to guarantee that the practice will help them to save or earn at least the amount of the additional fee, otherwise the firm will repay the difference to them. And it is a response that seems to work, since according to Gordon it has "helped us win two new clients in the last four weeks."

If clients cannot see the benefits, in spite of the guarantee, they simply opt for the scaled down "Basics" service, with a more "hands off " approach.

Improving service delivery

In addition to extending the range of services provided, Gordons Knight has also improved the way they are delivered and paid for.

One of the keys to this has been their in-house creation of a database tool that tracks every job from advance alert through to completion. This has several features that improve the efficient processing of each job, including:

- Automated reminders go to clients if information is missing or records are not received within 7 days of them being due.

- The relevant team member and the client automatically receive an email if a job is not progressed within a specified number of days, ensuring jobs aren't delayed unnecessarily.

- At the end of each job, the client receives a report that states the number of reminders they have received during the course of the job. Since the delays cause extra work, this report is used when negotiating fees for the following year.

In addition, all members of the administration team are now required to plan their work for the following day before they leave the office each night. And they are also required to focus on the more responsive active clients (rated A and B) before dealing with those on the "Basics" service or those that pay fees late and delay sending their information in until the last minute (rated C and D).

Credit control has also been tightened, with any clients not paying within 60 days of the due date being required to pay by standing order for subsequent years.

Innovative use of video

As a result of these efficiency improvements, most jobs are now completed within fifteen working days of receiving records. But Gordon's Knight is not content to stop there. So at the end of every accounts job they now record a screenshot video using the commercially available, and very easy to use, "Camtasia" software.

Essentially this software allows them to record whatever is on the screen of a computer, along with an accompanying audio track captured via a simple microphone. They therefore use it to pull up the client's accounts on screen and record a video talking through any outstanding issues and queries, providing a commentary, giving feedback and making suggestions for improvements.

The resulting video is then sent to the client so they can deal with the issues raised at a time that is convenient for them, as well as showing it to their bookkeeper, if relevant, to take any improvement suggestions on board.

"Feedback on these videos has been brilliant," says Gordon. "And, as it is a differentiation feature, it gives us a competitive edge and really gets us talked about. More importantly, it helps the client get more value from their investment in our service. After all, their success is closely followed by ours!"

"We are tireless in our search to offer more value and the best service. Our collection of regular feedback demonstrates that we are leading the field in terms of advice depth, speed and value," Gordon concludes.

Ground-breaking innovation creates much better life-work balance

GreenStones is a Peterborough based, 16 person practice with one principal, Simon Chaplin.

In some ways its story is one of the most ground-breaking, thought provoking and inspiring I have ever come across, for reasons that I think will become obvious as you read on...

Purpose and values

For Simon and his team, everything starts with their purpose and values. The purpose of the firm is striking:

"Inspiring, Challenging and Supporting colleagues and customers to be the best they can be."

"Those words, and their order, were very carefully chosen," explains Simon. "We start by trying to inspire people to do better, and get better results, in their businesses, jobs or lives. We give them examples of what is possible and show them how we have done it ourselves. Where that doesn't work, plan B is to challenge their beliefs and ask them why they haven't taken a particular action or implemented a particular idea. This is always a more difficult and less comfortable approach. Whichever way people choose to change they will always need support to go through that process and get the very best results."

The values of the firm are equally striking:

1. Help each other
2. Share relevant knowledge
3. Seek enjoyable balance
4. Be honest
5. Be brave

Simon comments: "At first I thought we had seven values, but when I was challenged to come up with real stories illustrating us doing the other two I couldn't, so I realised that they weren't actually the things that we lived by and we couldn't call them our values."

"In fact the process of illustrating our values proved to be so powerful that the team spent a whole away day identifying their favourite story for each of our five values. We then commissioned an artist to turn them into a comic book style storyboard that now has pride of place in every office and meeting room as a graphic reminder of what is most important to us."

Personal One Page Plans

Like many of the most successful practices, GreenStones have long used a business-wide monthly One Page Plan (BOPP) to measure, manage and improve the things that matter in their business. But some of the things they measure on it are very innovative, including:

- Number of "development activities" – "Which we define as anything that takes about an hour and helps you to do a better job – although we specifically exclude exam training and the CPD required by professional bodies, since that is a given, and we don't believe their standards go far enough for our purposes. By way of example, the latest figures (for the month of February 2011) were for a target of 34 and we actually achieved 43 development activities in the month."

- Number of "meaningful conversations" – these are unsolicited phone calls to customers that are genuinely proactive in nature (the target was 92 such phone calls, but they actually achieved 138 in February)

- Improvement ideas – the number generated and the number implemented

- Targets achieved – the % of the firm's 18 key targets that had been fully met or exceeded in the month (83% in February)

However, the real innovation comes in the way they have also created a monthly Personal One Page Plan ('POPP') for every single person in the business. Structurally these POPPs:

- Set numerical targets for each area of the team member's responsibility

- Measure actual performance in those areas

- Show actual performance as a percentage of the target

- Quantify the "Gap" between actual and target

- Present the last two items in both bar graph and spider diagram format for clarity

- Summarise the key actions taken this month to address the issues arising from the previous month's POPP

- List the agreed actions that the team member will take over the coming month to address the issues arising from this month's POPP

Obviously the things targeted and measured on the POPPs, vary from person to person, but are always very carefully thought through to align the behaviour of each team member with the desired outcomes for the firm as a whole. For example, they include:

- How happy customers are with the service they have received from that particular team member – based on random customer surveys using a 1-10 scale

- The monetary value of the extra work orders that have been generated on their customers – i.e. the extra work over and above the core services the firm normally supplies to these clients

- The number of development activities and meaningful conversations (i.e. as described above) that they have personally achieved

- Their average number of outstanding actions as shown on their control panel in the firm's IRIS Practice Management software, and

- How happy the rest of the team are with them – with the data being captured anonymously using a 1-10 scale

"Given our values, we decided to put all POPPs on a single spreadsheet so that everybody can see everybody else's every month, and that includes every team member seeing mine," explains Simon. "Yes it is brave, but by sharing relevant information in such an open and honest way, we can all help, inspire, challenge and support each other to be the best we can be. And that is what we are all about."

"Of course, to formalise that process, I also review every team member's POPP with them every month, and work with them to set their targets and create their action plans for the coming month. So I always have my finger on the pulse, and am always there to support them so that they, and the firm, get better and better results."

Investors In People Gold Award

The GreenStones approach to inspiring, challenging and supporting its team impressed the Investor In People assessors so much that they were granted the IIP Gold Award at their first attempt.

"To get this you have to meet 165 evidence requirements, compared to the 35 for standard IIP accreditation. Less than 1% of all IIP businesses have achieved Gold and I believe we were one of the first three financial businesses anywhere in the UK to get it. So, given that they see thousands of businesses, to be assessed as being in the top 1% makes us very proud and convinces us that we are on the right track."

Results Only Work Environment

Building on all this success, and fuelled by their values of bravery, helping each other and seeking an enjoyable balance, in late 2010, GreenStones embarked on its most ground-breaking innovation to date: a Results Only Work Environment, or ROWE.

Essentially, ROWE involves the business saying to its team members, "We don't care where you do it, or when you do it, as long as the work gets done to the right standard and by the right date." And the implications of that single sentence are profound:

- **Freedom** – Team members can come and go as they please, and work wherever they like – although obviously, meetings with customers must still be at an appropriate time and place that works for them. However, this could be 6.30 in the morning at the gym or 7.30 at night in the pub.

- **100% results focused** – The focus is now solely on the results of the practice and the individual.

- **Internal meetings made voluntary** – "The team said that sometimes they were not getting anything from the internal meetings, so we have now made every meeting voluntary and replaced them by using some fantastic online software called Rypple, which really has transformed how we communicate with and support each other."

- **Efficiency improvements benefit the team** – "Under the traditional model, if a team member works out how to do things more efficiently, and finishes their work for the day early at say 1pm, they will probably be given another job to do until home time. So really there is little incentive for them to improve things. But under ROWE, if they get better and finish at 1pm, they enjoy the benefits since they can go home if they want – if they even came to the office to start with!"

- **Unlimited holidays** – "Continuing my previous example, instead of going home at 1pm, imagine that they get ahead of themselves by staying at their desk and working on jobs we didn't expect them to do until later in the week. And if they keep doing that, and finish all of that month's work by half way through the month, they can take the second half of the month off as holiday, without any loss of pay or any erosion of their standard holiday entitlement. So, in effect, holidays become unlimited."

The payback

Admirable as this all sounds, is it actually paying off ? According to Simon the answer is a categoric yes:

- **Financial payback** – "Over the last two years turnover has increased by 19%, net profits have increased by 45%, whilst team costs as a proportion of turnover have fallen from 50.1% to 46.5%. I understand that if we benchmark the team costs to turnover ratio against other firms it would not be great, but what that ratio does not show is the standard of service we give to our customers, the fact I do not work Friday afternoons and that I had 13 weeks holiday last year. Average rejections (internal mistakes) per job have reduced from 2 to 1.1, and referrals received from customers have doubled from 2 a month to 4. Customer happiness has remained constant at an average of 9.3 out of 10."

- **Non financial payback** – "There is a real buzz about the place. Customers are getting superb service and they are getting it quickly. The team is feeling really valued and revelling in the extra flexibility and responsibility. As for me, I am extremely proud and extremely happy. I am also really excited about what the future holds."

As for the impact of ROWE, that is still very much in its infancy, but the early signs are very promising: "Since we introduced it we have been hitting a higher percentage of our One Page Plan targets than ever before, so far from being an indulgence, it does genuinely seem to be making a very positive contribution."

How to use seminars to grow your practice

In this, a second example of excellence from GreenStones, Peterborough based sole practitioner Simon Chaplin explains how the firm uses seminars to win new clients and earn additional fees from existing clients.

For several years GreenStones had used the monthly Business Builder Forum (BBF) CDs from AVN as the core material for their monthly business club meetings. Typically they had between 10 and 20 people attending each month, with six regulars paying £50 per month and the others coming as guests.

Club meetings were structured to start at breakfast time with a 45-60 minute presentation on a key business topic using the ready-to-use slides and other material on the BBF CD, followed by a break for coffee, and then resuming with a "Strategic Board" session where members used their combined experience and expertise to help each other to solve their pressing problems.

According to MD Simon Chaplin: "These events were a real success, helping us to enhance our reputation as business advisers, add value to our existing clients so that they were more loyal, gave us more referrals and bought additional services, and convert more of our prospects into clients. They were also really enjoyable to run. But eventually we decided we needed to shake things up a little to prevent it becoming stale."

Making running seminars much easier

From September 2008 they made two big changes. Firstly, they switched from a monthly to a quarterly cycle. And secondly, instead of the presenters being from the GreenStones team, (MD Simon Chaplin and Customer Manager Mark Wrigley) they began hiring nationally-recognised keynote speakers. To help differentiate the new version from the old, they also changed the name to the "Grow Your Business Forum."

So far the keynote speakers have included:

- Will Kintish on how to increase sales and profits by becoming much better at networking

- Philip Hesketh on the psychology of influence and persuasion

- Paul Shrimpling on how to use One Page Plans to make better business decisions and get better business results

- Michael Heppell on how to be brilliant

- And me, Steve Pipe, on how one small business owner added £2.3 million to their business and personal bank account by using a Performance Measurement and Improvement (PMI) system, and how GreenStones could help delegates do the same in their businesses

As a result of these changes, with more time between events, and free from the need to prepare and practise the content, they have been able to concentrate on getting more paying delegates to attend each event. The main techniques they use for filling the room are:

- The next event is always promoted heavily at the end of each event, so the marketing cycle effectively lasts three months.

- An A5 flyer is professionally designed and sent to all customers at every opportunity.

- Details of the forum are posted on the website and promoted via Twitter, Linkedin and Facebook.

- A5 flyers are distributed at all networking meetings.

- Details are added to all team members' email signatures so they don't have to remember to ask customers.

Commenting on the impact of the changes, Simon Chaplin said: "They have made our life much easier. It is much easier to organise 4 events a year than it is 12. It's much easier to fill the room. It's much easier to get non-clients along to hear a well-known speaker than it is to hear what they assume will be a boring accountant. And it is much easier to recoup your event costs because it's much easier to get delegates to pay."

"It is also much easier to prepare and practise a short Chairman's introduction and wrap up than it is an entire 60 minute presentation. It's much easier to focus on looking after delegates on the day when you aren't distracted by your speaking duties. And it's much easier to follow up afterwards."

Getting much better results

By way of example, here is what happened at the quarterly seminar that I had the pleasure of being the keynote speaker for:

- 35 delegates attended – with most paying £50 plus VAT to be there

- 20 separate businesses were represented – including three potential new clients

- 15 of the businesses present ticked a box on the feedback form saying they wanted to pay £250 for a meeting with GreenStones to discuss the issues raised at the seminar. So the practice lined up an extra £3,750 in immediate meeting fees, and no doubt much more to follow as a result of the extra services to be discussed at the meetings

- Two of the three prospects requested a meeting to become a client

- One existing client wanted to talk seriously about some advanced EBT-based profit extraction planning featured in the seminar that will generate very substantial tax saving for the client and a very substantial value based fee for the practice

- Another long-standing client has already signed up for monthly One Page Plan meetings at £6,000 per annum

- And 25 tickets were sold on the day, at £147 each, for the next quarterly seminar

Commenting on the results, Simon Chaplin said: "Yes it takes effort to make our events a success, but these results speak for themselves. Not only do they represent a really superb immediate return on our investment. But they also give us the very real prospect of eye-watering additional fees in the future. And remember, we achieved all of this in the middle of the January tax return season, which is traditionally a bad time for practice development."

Speed, proactivity and value for money

Ten years ago Stockport based Hallidays was a traditional practice employing around 35 people, turning over just over £1 million, and having about 180 days of work locked up in WIP and debtors. In addition, the partners worked very long hours, and struggled to take their annual holiday entitlement.

Today the eight partner firm has a team of around 60 people, is much more profitable, turns over almost £3 million, has almost eliminated lock up as a result of collecting most of its fees in advance by direct debit and standing orders, and a flexi time arrangement means that if partners work overtime they get up to 42 days (i.e. 7.5 working weeks) holiday a year. In addition, they were also recently named as the Accountancy Age medium sized firm of the year.

Managing partner Nigel Bennett says that the transformation started when they went on a couple of courses run by a network of accountants. "Those courses, and the network of forward thinking accountants they introduced us to (AVN), were the catalyst since they opened our minds to the fact that there was a better way to do things."

And according to Nigel, there have been six keys to the transformation of their practice and its results in the intervening years.

Pricing differently

"The first thing we did was stop using timesheets for pricing," says Nigel. Instead they now:

- Use pricing software to agree fixed price agreements in advance with every single client, so clients never receive a surprise bill

- Collect payment in advance by monthly direct debits

- Give a money back guarantee so that if a client isn't happy with what the firm has done for them in a month they can pay whatever amount they feel is fair for that month. "Although, in reality, hardly anyone ever triggers the guarantee, so we are never really out of pocket because of it. Quite the opposite in fact, since it helps us to win a lot of extra clients."

"It is fair to say that this approach to pricing has transformed our P&L account and balance sheet," says Nigel.

Systemising their Practice DNA

"We wanted to run our practice differently, using key performance indicators ('KPIs') instead of timesheets to drive things. But there was no software in the market at the time that did that, so we created our own," explains Nigel.

In addition to the things done by traditional practice management systems, Hallidays' 'Practice DNA' software ('PDNA') includes:

- KPI reporting and analysis

- Client grading and Pareto analysis

- Customer care systems that specify how many times they must proactively contact each client (e.g. A clients must be contacted every month, B clients every quarter etc)

- Meeting action plans

- To do lists, many of which are automatically populated by the customer care and other related systems from within the software

- Fixed Price Agreement and Extra Work Order generation and monitoring (in development)

- Team happiness measurement

- Flexi-time recording – flexi time means team members can earn up to 12 extra days off a year. "It has proved extremely popular" says Nigel. "And contrary to fears in some quarters, has not caused any loss of productivity."

Internally, this approach has greatly improved efficiency. For example, when it was introduced the average accounts job took 65 days to complete. Now that figure is just 25 days. And as a result the ratio of direct costs to turnover has improved significantly, with obvious consequences for profitability.

Focusing on three key issues

Instead of flitting between various "flavour of the month" issues, the primary focus of the business for the last ten years has consistently been on measuring, understanding and improving three key things that clients really care about:

1. **Proactivity** – This is measured by the PDNA system as the number of proactive contacts made as a result of the client care system. Interestingly, the introduction of this system also led to a 56% increase in the amount of extra work being generated from the firm's clients over and above the value of their fixed price agreements. "What we have found is that when we contact our clients proactively we develop a trusted advisor status more quickly and as a result they are more comfortable requesting additional services," says Nigel.

2. **Speed of response** – Turnaround times are measured automatically by the PDNA system for every single piece of work absolutely and against specified targets.

3. **Perceived value for money** – This is measured through a customer survey system triggered by PDNA. This system encompasses postal, email and telephone surveys carried out every month on a rotating basis. The clients to survey are randomly generated by PDNA.

"Our performance in all of these three areas is then automatically reported back to either the individual teams or the business as a whole via our One Page Plan. There, it is also compared to our targets, and used to identify corrective action where necessary," explains Nigel.

Improved communications

Communication amongst the partners has been transformed by holding carefully structured:

- Annual strategy meetings to decide on the big picture issues

- Quarterly partner meetings to hold each other to account on big picture issues and actions

- Fortnightly partner meetings to discuss day to day issues

In addition, weekly meetings for individual teams, and monthly firm-wide meetings at which the One Page Plan is discussed, ensure that the entire team is up to speed on everything that matters.

Better systems to win new clients and new fees

"We have worked hard to improve the systems we use to win new clients," says Nigel. Some of the most successful things they now do with prospects include:

- Running five 'Business Builder Forum' seminars a year to prove that the firm can help them to manage, lead, develop and grow their businesses – with a carefully thought out seating plan so that prospects are sat next to 'raving fans' of the firm

- Using PDNA to systemise the process of staying in touch with prospects so that, when they are ready to buy, Hallidays is on the tip of their tongues. There are two tracks to this system – one for warmer leads, and a more relaxed one for colder leads

- Pitching for work with a 'Heart selling' questioning system. "Instead of droning on and on about us, as some accountants do, we let the prospect do most of the talking by using questions to uncover all the business's needs and wants, and getting them to articulate why those things are important," explains Nigel. "And when they have finished, instead of us telling them about everything we could do for them, we only tell them about the things that specifically match their requirements. Using this approach gets us much higher conversion rates, since the meetings are 100% focused on them and their needs rather than us and ours."

- Using pricing software and offering guarantees also make a big difference to conversion rates. "People really like the fact that our software makes the pricing process fair, by making it open and transparent and eliminating surprise bills. And they are also much more likely to accept a fee proposal higher than they are being quoted elsewhere because the guarantee means that they will never end up paying more than they feel our help was actually worth."

- As part of the sales pitch they also explain that as soon as they become a client they will get a half day meeting – the aim of which is to fully understand what their business and personal goals are so that everything Hallidays does for them is done with those goals in mind

The best referral systems

Like many successful firms, Hallidays have always regarded referrals from clients and introducers as the best source of new work. So they have set up a full suite of systems for generating referrals, and measuring their success at doing so.

As a result Nigel has discovered that: "Client happiness surveys are one of the best ways to generate referrals. In our surveys we always ask, on a scale of 1-10, how willing they are to refer their contacts to us. If the score is below an 8 we ask them what we are doing wrong, and then move mountains to put things right. And if the score is 8 or above we ask them who they would like to refer to us next. It's a very simple and very powerful way to improve service and get more referrals."

Impact of the recession

The firm has taken the recession in its stride. As Nigel explains: "Our turnover growth has been modest over the last two years. We have of course lost some clients, but we have been able to replace them with better clients. So the firm has continued to operate on a stable financial basis and we are still pleased with our progress."

And it is not only the partners who are pleased with the firm's progress: "Despite not giving anyone a pay rise for two years – although we have paid bonuses based on the results of the business – team happiness as measured monthly by our PDNA software is at an all time high. So clearly our people are as keen as we are on the way the firm is going."

A three pronged approach to serving clients

According to partner Glyn Davison, Harlands decided to "help its clients to ride the economic storm and try and avoid the recession." As a result, most of those clients have made it through a distinctly challenging period. And the practice's own results have never been better, including:

- Fee income from existing clients has increased by 33% in the last 17 months

- Client referrals have hit the highest number since the firm was founded

- The partners now work an average of 42 hours a week

- The firm was named as the North East Independent Firm of the Year in 2010

This six-partner practice, with offices in Newcastle upon Tyne and Consett, has achieved its success by seeking to become more than traditional accountants. "We aim to affect the result and not just report on the score," explains Glyn. "We offer a comprehensive accountancy and financial planning service to business owners, the sole aim of which is to increase their profit and develop their wealth. Over the past couple of years, as the recession has deepened, we have also had to work further on protecting their profit and wealth."

Three pronged approach to serving clients

Harland's emphasis is on working closely with its clients to ensure it has the maximum effect on their business. This effort is focused on three distinct areas:

1. **Saving clients money** – through core accountancy and tax services such as tax planning and cashflow planning and management (see the next section for details)

2. **Making clients money** – through business improvement advice and support such as ensuring sustainability in uncertain times, increasing sales, improving profit, obtaining funding and helping them to write tender documents

3. **Developing their wealth** – through proper financial planning, so that they invest wisely and plan carefully

Although this methodology has brought substantial financial gains for the practice and its clients, it isn't just about money, as Glyn confirms: "Value isn't just financial for our clients — this is a given. They especially value the improvements in their lifestyle that our input helps them to enjoy. Lifestyle value can be measured by such things as the ability to automate their business systems which results in extra time they are able to spend with family and friends. Or, in some situations, just being able to continue in the current economic conditions with less daily worries and stress. And in many cases it is absolutely priceless to them."

Helping clients with their cashflow planning and management

"In a recession cash is king," says Glyn. "So a key focus of our work in the last few years has been to help clients understand their current cash position, forecast what it is going to be in the future, and help them create a plan and take action to fill in any shortfalls."

They do this through a cashflow forecasting service, some of the main features of which are:

- It is a fixed price service, with the size of the fee depending on factors such as the quality of the client's record. For example, a typical fee for a small company with up to date accounts would be in the region of £500-£1000 a year

- Detailed 2-3 year forecasts are produced cost effectively using Sage's Winforecast software

- The annual fee usually includes two or three short meetings a year with the client

- Benchmarking software is also used to see how the client compares to others in their industry, and to identify where the evidence suggests there may be the greatest scope for improvement

- Where necessary, detailed corrective action plans are developed, and

- The results are shared with, and explained to, the client's bank and other key third parties in order to ensure they stay on board

According to Glyn "One of the most important things we do at our cashflow meetings is to use 'What If ?' analysis to educate clients. For example, many have no idea how damaging it can be to their cashflow if their debtor days figure is allowed to creep up by 5 days. So we spend a lot of time making that sort of thing clear, which is often a revelation to them. And by focussing on worst-case scenarios we are able to help clients develop really robust plans to create more headroom and prevent cashflow becoming a problem."

"Although worst-case 'What If' analysis has become much more important during the recession, we still always look for the positives too," says Glyn. "So we also use our Business Potential profit sensitivity software to show clients how much better their sales and margins can be if they make a number of small and manageable improvements to such factors as their sales lead generation rates, sales lead conversion rates, average prices charged, average amount customers spend and the average number of times they buy from the business in a year. We can then factor those sorts of sales and margin improvements into the cashflow projection to show clients the impact there too. And again it is usually a revelation that makes clients really determined to make those sorts of improvements happen."

In addition to being invaluable for clients, this systematic approach to cashflow planning has also been a key driver of the firm's growth during the recession. "As well as the direct fees for the cashflow forecasting itself, a lot of clients also ask us to help them implement the things on their resulting action plans. And that means we earn extra fees for that extra work too. And with over 30 clients using the service, the amounts really add up."

Getting the best from the team

"Each client has a client manager as well as a partner," explains Phil Murray, Marketing and Customer Service Director. "That person is focused on the individual needs of the client and co-ordinating our services to ensure the maximum effect on their businesses. This gives the team the opportunity to grow their skills sets and get closer to clients, allowing the partners to work less in the business and more on the business."

All managers and partners also now have mobile phones with email capability to ensure that clients can always get in touch with them and that response times are reduced.

And because the firm has also focused on developing the profit and wealth improvement abilities of its people, the team is able to do a lot of the work involved in helping clients achieve their goals in these areas. As a result, the partners have been freed up to concentrate on other projects, from which they have been able to generate very significant additional fees.

When combined with other improvements to the firm's systems, these changes have also improved efficiency, and consequently have helped to reduce the average working week of the team to 37 hours, and of the partners to 42 hours a week.

Winning clients with social networking

Harland has enthusiastically embraced the concept of social networking, both for keeping in touch with existing clients and for marketing purposes. Phil says: "We have encouraged the team to use social media to interact with clients and potential clients. We also advertise our free Business Builder seminars on Facebook, Linked In and Twitter and we have got more than £45,000 of recurring fees directly from Facebook and Twitter recently, with a further £20,000 quoted right now from this source."

The practice's commitment to social networking has led to it spreading the word to the local business community, as Phil explains: "As a direct result of demand by clients, we have been running social media workshops and awareness workshops, which have attracted more than 400 guests to the events. Furthermore, we also ran a follow-up full day on social media training, which is fully funded by the government. This has seen our new client appointments increase dramatically by upwards of 40% in two months."

Being more professional and commercial leads to a 29% increase in turnover in a year

In 2010 Harvey Smith & Co, an eight person practice in Essex led by sole practitioner Alan Cowperthwaite, increased its turnover by 29%. According to Alan, most of that improvement is a consequence of "being even more professional in the way we help clients, and being even more commercial in the way we price for that help."

Getting it right with incorporations

As an example of being more professional, he has introduced a new system whereby every time his team produces a set of accounts for an unincorporated business, they run the numbers through their Incorporation Tax Planner software to see whether there are any potential tax savings from incorporation. And if there are, the team uses the software to produce a plain English report that Alan can discuss with the client.

This may not seem like rocket science, but the straw polls I have conducted with over 500 accountants at my recent seminars suggest that less than 5% of practices even claim to do this. Of course, most of the firms surveyed say they do it some of the time with some of their clients. But less than 5% claim to do it every year with every client. And yet one or more of the client's profits, drawings aspirations, attitude and tax regime may well have changed. So surely we have a professional responsibility to consider it every year for every unincorporated client?

Winning when other firms don't get it right

Alan's systematic approach to giving professional incorporation advice is not only paying dividends with existing clients. It is also helping him to win good quality new clients, as he explains:

"A sole trader with a highly respected professional qualification, and seven employees, was referred to me. He had been with his accountant for a long time, but had never been advised to consider incorporating. So when I met him, I opened up our Incorporation Tax Planner software and showed him that he could save about £28,000 a year in tax by incorporating, with a further c. £70,000 over the next five years or so if he also capitalised goodwill.

I think he was shell-shocked, and astounded that he had never been given that advice before. After all, by not giving him this advice years ago, his accountant had literally cost him tens of thousands of pounds.

I then went on to use our pricing software to show him how much our 3, 4 and 5 star services would cost him. There was an audible gulp when he saw the 4 star price of £5,500, since he had previously been paying only £2,000 for what was notionally a very similar service. But, even so, he appointed us there and then because he knew that we were going to leave no stone unturned in serving him properly, and that the fee was tiny compared to the value we would bring.

I should also stress that the £5,500 agreed fee is only for the ongoing annual work. I will be having a separate conversation with him in due course about the fee for helping him to incorporate."

All of that was very professional. But what impressed me even more was that immediately afterwards Alan called a meeting to debrief his team on why the other accountant had lost this client by letting them down, and to re-focus their energies so that Harvey Smith & Co never lost a client in a similar way. In my opinion it is that sort of attention to detail that is the mark of a true professional. And it is therefore no surprise that the practice is enjoying such success.

Pricing more commercially

According to Alan, the second key to their 29% growth rate is that they now set their prices more commercially. And there are two main elements to this: their pricing methodology and the actual prices they charge.

Their new pricing methodology involves using software to give clients a choice of three different service bundles:

- 3 Star – which covers the basic compliance work
- 4 Star – which adds in tax planning, and
- 5 Star – which is more all singing and all dancing.

Rather than just take last year's fee and add a bit for inflation, they also took a long hard look at the current fee every client was paying, and used their new methodology to arrive at a proper commercial fee. Where this was significantly more than the historical fee, they then had a one to one meeting with the client to explain that the fees were too low and that out of fairness they needed to be adjusted. And, as Alan explains, the results of this process were very positive:

"Even though we were in the jaws of a recession, pretty much the only clients we lost were the smaller ones where we had never priced properly. All our good clients stayed. And some of the fee increases were pretty big. For example, I had one client where the fee went up from £2,000 to £4,000 and he said to me afterwards that it was still 'very reasonable', and another where due to their growth, the fee went up from £1,500 to £7,000 and he settled it the very next day. So our experience is that when you serve clients properly, and explain the situation carefully, fee resistance melts away."

A sole practitioner who added £600,000 to his turnover in just five years

Mark Hollyman is a sole practitioner in his mid 40s. He started ISIS in 2005 with £300k in fees and in what he describes as a "nondescript" small town, Wellingborough in Northamptonshire. By 2010 he had around 200 clients, was employing fewer people than in 2005 (9 including him and his wife), and was turning over more than £900k. As a result he was posting annual profits of between £400,000 and £500,000.

Here in his own words is how Mark explained his success to me in June 2010.

Without being arrogant, we have always been genuinely excellent on compliance and service. That is the bedrock. Get that right and everything else follows. But what we do now is blowing away the competition.

The great thing about being an accountant is that you don't have to sell anything. Because of your compliance excellence, clients trust you. And from that trust, it all falls into place.

It is not about winning new clients (in fact, I don't need to win any new clients for a few years). It is about serving the existing ones better. Because when you do, they ask you to do more and more for them. That is how we have grown.

Our profession is woefully letting down its clients by not keeping pace with their needs and demands. Over the next ten years there will be a fundamental shift as ageing practitioners leave the marketplace and others come in who are determined to look forward rather than merely looking back.

The key is to look forward. To help them create a much better future. With much better profits. Much better cashflow. Much better tax bills. And much better wealth.

It is such a refreshing change from what most accountants do, that banks and business owners are blown away.

Looking forward through seminars

As an example, a few months ago 20 businesses came to a seminar we ran that showed them how to improve their profits, cashflow, tax position and family wealth.

18 of them ticked a box on the feedback form asking to pay us £250 for a follow up meeting to discuss the issues raised at the seminar. In addition to the £4,500 in meeting fees, the benefits to us so far have included:

- A Lloyds bank manager was so impressed that he started giving us many more referrals. Two of those alone will create £20-30k in fees for us. He also got us in front of the group managers and directors, and I now have a standing invitation to go back regularly to update them. And from that I was invited to present to the key people at their national invoice discounting arm in Oxford, and am now getting leads from across the country from them.

- Two delegates asked us to introduce them to a tax boutique that can help them set up relatively small EFRBS, from which we will earn over £30,000. NB: Our fees are at this level since in addition to the normal payaways we receive from the tax boutique, we also charge clients an extra fee on top for the support we provide to them e.g. if the tax boutique charges 7%, we round that up to 10% and keep the extra 3% as our support fee. In addition we charge trustee fees of c. £1,500, and we also get a share of the 7% charged by the boutique. So in total, when we work with a tax boutique, we typically get to keep c. 40-50% of what the client pays (and, of course, if we don't work with a tax boutique we keep 100% of what the client pays).

Knowing what I know now, I would have invested three times as much energy into getting people to attend the seminar. And I would have made sure we had a lot more capacity to follow up afterwards, since we haven't been able to do as much of that as I would have liked.

But even so the payback from that one seminar alone has already been over £60,000, and there is still a lot more follow up to do.

The keys to success with advanced tax planning

Linking up with tax boutiques in order to be to be able to offer advanced tax planning is also very powerful. In my experience the keys to making it work really well are:

- Tell prospects about the advanced tax planning solutions they will be able to access through you. And quantify the savings the solutions could help them to achieve, since that is what really impresses and excites them. (This last bit applies equally to clients too).

- Recognise that advanced tax planning can be a Trojan horse strategy with prospects. Be happy if at first, out of loyalty to their existing accountant, they only want you to help them with advanced tax planning. They will probably ask to switch the rest of their affairs to you within a year or so, once they realise that sticking with an ordinary accountant is actually costing them a lot more than just the fee.

- Don't feel constrained by the tax boutique's suggested pricing structure. Instead regard those as minimum prices, and if you feel that with your involvement and in your market the work is worth more, ask the boutique to charge more in your market and pay the price premium over to you.

- Don't be constrained by geography either. For example, we are currently in the middle of the largest ever retrospective additional capital allowances claim on land and buildings our tax boutique has ever done. And it is for a £4m care home about 100 miles away on the South Coast. By bringing together a multidisciplinary team to properly reclassify what the client actually bought for their £4m, we have been able to identify an extra £1m in capital allowances that had never previously been claimed. So not only will the client be hundreds of thousands of pounds better off, but our share of the fees generated will be in the region of £40,000.

Other keys to our success

Other examples of the things we do that really make a difference include:

- Although I no longer personally keep timesheets, the team do in order to be able to 'sanity check' our fees. As for how we calculate our fees, we use value billing where possible, but still do some time based billing where we have to. Either way, we are never cheap, since a premium service must be matched with a premium price. But what we have found is that price resistance melts away when you do the right things. So my belief is that price resistance is self inflicted pain – i.e. something that firms meet when they are not doing enough of the right things for clients

- Introducing direct debits. We have found that clients are very happy to pay our fees that way, and are also keen to use direct debits with their customers. So they are helping to transform the cashflow of our business and of our clients' businesses too

- Building on our newly strengthened links with Lloyds we recently launched a 'Funding Finding' service whereby we charge clients 5-10% to help them find funds. Often it only involves a few calls to our banking contacts and a few hours work by a team member using benchmarking, trend analysis and sensitivity software, to show why they are a lendable proposition. Five years ago there was no need for this type of service. But now it is invaluable, and clients are happy to pay for it since they only ask for help when all else has failed.

My motivation

For me it is not about money. But neither is profit a dirty word. As a senior professional and job-creating entrepreneur I deserve to be well rewarded. And as a father and husband I am determined not to earn those rewards in a way that sacrifices the things that are precious to me.

So I now only work about 30 hours week (I cannot be more precise since I no longer keep timesheets). And I use all my extra time to do things that leave a legacy and make my life fulfilling.

I want to leave a legacy to my family as a good father and husband. I want to leave a legacy to my community, which is why I am heavily involved in local politics as a councillor. And I want to have 'me time' for my hobbies, such as shooting, and all the other things I really enjoy.

Recruiting , treating and paying the team properly

Simultaneously serving clients extraordinarily well, working 30 hours a week and earning very high profits is only possible because of the decisions we made in respect of our team. In particular:

- We are deliberately very top heavy with lots of senior people

- We only recruit exceptionally good people who, in addition to impeccable technical knowledge, also have people skills, and the ability to handle complaints, resolve problems and spot opportunities

- One of the main reasons they choose to join us is because we pay exceptionally well

The main reasons they choose to stay with us are:

- We genuinely empower them, making them responsible for the entire client relationship

- Clients are very happy with this, since in our sales and marketing we make it clear that it is the business that will serve them, not me personally

- I only get involved in their client relationships by exception – i.e. when I am really needed

- In a sense we throw them in at the deep end, with lots of challenges and responsibilities as befits them as senior professionals

- But we do not throw them in the deep end with a block of concrete around their feet. Instead we give them the systems, support and tools they need to stay afloat

- And I say to them "If you are ambitious, talk to me and I'll help", since I would much rather find a way of accommodating their ambition, instead of frustrating it and see them leave. And I can tell you this approach pays dividends. For example, because of it I am about to open a second office in 50:50 partnership with an ambitious 28 year old employee who wanted to move up. That kind of arrangement is much better for me (and him) than see him leave to set up a rival practice

Fee growth of 32% in one year, and 10 new pieces of profitable work in one day

In February 2011 Andrew James of James Stanley & Co stood up in front of over 50 of his clients at Edgbaston Golf Club and proudly explained that he had grown his firm's turnover by 32% in the last year.

His clients were delighted for him, and as a result paid even more attention to the seminar Andrew was hosting that day, on the basis that "if Andrew and his team can get those sorts of results for their business in the jaws of a recession, perhaps they can help us get better results too."

And by the end of the seminar, Birmingham based sole practitioner Andrew and his team of eight people had signed up 10 new pieces of profitable work, and had received five referrals and 14 other hot leads to follow up.

A seminar that delivers for clients

As the results suggest, this was no ordinary seminar. It ran from 9.30 until 1pm, and at its heart was a case study of how Dave, a small business owner turning over £100,000 at the start of the story, got an extra £2.3 million net of all taxes and costs over 25 years of working with a really good accountant.

That sort of amount of extra cash almost sounds too good to be true, and no doubt it also seemed that way to the audience at the outset. But their scepticism disappeared very quickly. Since, as each chapter in Dave's story was explained, the audience were shown what he did and how much extra net cash flowed into his bank account as a consequence, and heard how they could achieve equivalent (although potentially larger) inflows into their own bank accounts by doing the same sort of things Dave did.

The speaker also went to great lengths to make it clear that none of the extra cash came from any kind of investments, financial products, stocks and shares or property. Instead it all came from really good business common sense, financial discipline and tax planning. In other words from all the things clients should expect a really good accountant to be helping them with.

Specifically, all of the extra £2.3 million was achieved by a really good accountant helping with:

- Incorporating the business, capitalising goodwill, and claiming tax credits while drawing down the resulting loan account

- Further profit extraction planning once the loan account has been repaid

- Creating a mathematically precise "Success Driver Map" of Dave's business model to see exactly what drives the profitability of the business, using it to measure the impact of new ideas, and building the ideas that work into the business's systems

- Benchmarking the business against others in the industry to see what else is possible

- Using sensitivity software to help him to understand the positive impact of increasing his prices

- Creating a monthly One Page Plan that gave Dave all the financial and non financial information he needed to get better results by making better decisions and having his finger firmly on the pulse of everything that matters

- Using LLP based planning to effectively pay no tax on the first five years of expansion profits he earns when he launches a major new business alongside his existing business

- Legitimately reclassifying much of the cost of buying a commercial property for the business so that he receives greatly increased capital allowances

- Making the business more valuable when he retires by making it more profitable and professionally run

- IHT and care fee planning for Dave and his wife's parents, and an elderly Aunt who also wants to leave her estate to them

- And various other kinds of tax planning

There was no rocket science in most of this. But the combined impact on Dave's bank account adds up, even after deducting all taxes and costs, to a staggering £2.3 million over the 25 years until he retires at 65.

Most accountants have no idea that, by leaving no stone unturned, they can make this kind of profound difference to the lives of even very small clients.

Neither do most business owners. So by showing them the facts in this way, the seminar really grabs their attention and makes them excited about achieving similar results for themselves. Which is why, by the end of the seminar, so many of the delegates were ready to start paying Andrew and his team to make a start.

How it also delivers for the practice

At its peak around 70 people had booked to attend. Inevitably, though, some of them cancelled, and some no-showed.

Of course, it is likely that if people had paid to attend rather than getting their places for free, a lower proportion would have dropped out. On the other hand, had it not been free it is likely that fewer people would have booked in the first place. So Andrew took the strategic decision to not to make price an issue for people, and therefore invited them to come for free as his guests.

On the day there were around 50 delegates in the room from 33 different businesses. And of those:

- 10 ticked a box at the end of the seminar saying that they wanted to pay £250 for Andrew and his team to benchmark them, carry out a diagnostic review of their affairs to see which parts of the seminar were most relevant to their situation, and then to have a meeting to help them draw up an action plan based on the findings

- A further 14 ticked a box saying that, in the first instance, they wanted to talk to the practice about one or more of the things covered during the seminar

As Andrew says: "Even taken at face value that is a great result for us. But, in addition, the feedback scores for the seminar itself were excellent, and the impression we made on the bankers and other introducers present, was first class. So I know there are going to be some very nice referrals coming our way too."

"The £250 we are charging for the bundle of services may not sound like a very big figure, but it is actually profitable on two levels," explains Andrew.

"Firstly even at £250, we make a profit on the bundle because we use benchmarking software and the OnTrack diagnostic review software to do the research at the push of a button – leaving most of the budget to fund a really high quality 2 hour action planning meeting."

"And secondly what usually happens at those meetings is that clients ask us to help them implement their action plans. In other words they ask us to do extra work, for which we charge extra fees. So we benefit twice. And it is the same with the 14 other clients that have asked to talk to us – many of those will go on to ask us to do extra work for them too."

The other keys to their 32% growth

Seminars like this are only one of the things James Stanley & Co have done in the last 18 months to transform the results of their practice. They have extended their range of services to include all the tax and business advisory issues covered by the seminar. They have become much more commercial in the way they calculate and collect their fees: using "Times Up" pricing software live in front of clients to show them how much things will cost, and using direct debits to get paid with much less hassle. And they have started to get the word out into the market that they are different in all these ways.

In Andrew's opinion: "The 32% growth we have enjoyed in the last 12 months is only the start. It is clear to us that what we are doing now, is what good clients and prospects want us to do. So by meeting more of their needs, more of them want to work with us, and they are happy to pay us more in fees."

Stop moaning and start doing something to make things better

Jason Blackman is an East Sussex based sole practitioner with one part time team member. By the end of 2010 he had just over 100 clients, many of whom were very small and paying very low fees. As a result Jason was working over 50 hours a week doing almost everything himself, and earning much less than he wanted to.

In late 2010 he started trying to improve his client base and the size of his average fees, but met with little success. So in early 2011 he spent a few hours with another sole practitioner who explained how he had successfully overcome the same challenge.

"That meeting was a catalyst," explained Jason. "Talking to someone who had faced the same problems, and hearing how they had transformed their life by changing their practice was hugely motivating. It gave me the insights, energy and courage I needed to do the same."

The three step approach he used to improve his lot was as follows:

STEP 1   Initially he graded all his clients using an A to E rating scheme, and then made the strategic decision only to continue working with A grade clients i.e. the "ideal" clients who perfectly fitted the profile of the practice he was trying to build.

STEP 2   In 2010 Jason had invested in some market leading accountancy pricing software, but had never really dared to use it, fearing that the prices it suggested were so much higher than he had traditionally charged. But on the advice of the sole practitioner who had inspired him, Jason now decided to not only use it with every single one of his A grade clients, but also to use the default prices in the software without making any downwards adjustments.

"The results have far exceeded my expectations," says Jason. "Every single one of my A grade clients has been happy to pay me the much higher fees calculated by the pricing software in return for me being able to give them more attention and a better service. In fact they have been incredibly positive about it."

STEP 3   Emboldened by the reaction from his A grade clients, Jason then explained to his other clients that the practice was changing and that it was probably no longer the best option for them, and that he would therefore like to introduce them to someone more suitable. Not only were his clients happy to switch to a potentially cheaper accountant, but that accountant was very pleased to pay Jason a market rate GRF multiple for the block of fees.

According to Jason: "I now earn higher total profits on my remaining 20 A grade clients than I used to earn from my entire 100+ client base at the turn of the year. And that is not all. Because I no longer have to serve the other 80 clients, I have freed up enough time to serve my clients better, start winning more grade A clients and also to have a better work-life balance. So it has given me a wonderful triple whammy of benefits."

"I believe," says Jason, "there were three keys to this turnaround in my fortunes. Firstly, inspiration, which I got from the practitioner who mentored me. Secondly, I had to stop moaning and actually do something, which took courage. And thirdly I used a proven process based on proven client grading and pricing tools from AVN. My only regret is that I didn't do all of this ages ago!"

Thriving when illness forces business partner to retire with just 3 hours notice

This case study was written by Robert Brown FCA, the owner of what was originally a two partner practice in Toddington. It tells the story of how the practice not only survived but actually thrived in the face of a cruel quirk of fate that would have destroyed many firms.

To put the story in context, the firm now turns over about £800,000, has average fees per client of around £6,000 and the principal takes 10 weeks holiday a year.

In October 2007 I went to a two day practice improvement conference with my then business partner. We had an excellent two days and began sketching out the new and exciting things we were going to do to strengthen our practice as a result of what we had heard and had been prompted to think about.

Exactly one week later my business partner of 12 years announced to me and our team that she had just been diagnosed with a very serious illness which would require an intensive course of treatment over the coming 2 months.

She passed her in-tray across the desk and, to cut a long story short, never returned to Landers.

Happily my partner, Finola McManus, went on to fight and win her own battle with typical resolve and success.

We were, at that stage, a team of 12 people. I effectively found myself in the position of being a sole trader, a trading style for which I have the utmost respect, but I know it isn't for me!

So to put it very bluntly, I confess to feeling more than a little daunted at what lay ahead.

We are now more successful than ever

Looking back now, more than 3 years later, I need not have worried. Landers, I am glad to say, continues to thrive as a practice with more team members and a stable and growing client base, growing turnover and growing total profit. Further more, I do not work more than 37 hours a week, and have still managed to take 10 weeks holiday in the last 12 months.

What is more, we achieved all of this despite what the IMF have described as "the worst recession in 60 years"... and despite the suddenness of Finola's departure and the potential gaping hole, that might have resulted in any other business collapsing by the loss of a co-owner and such a key driver.

So how did we do it?

I believe there are 3 fundamental reasons why we have been able to adapt, survive and thrive as a business, despite a potentially devastating blow, and in a challenging commercial environment. And within those three areas I think it is also possible to identify the 30 or so specific actions that have made a huge difference.

Success Factor 1 – People

The loss of my partner meant I was faced with a clear choice for absorbing the extra workload. At one extreme I could double my personal working week – completely unsustainable. The alternative was to involve our team – which is the path I chose.

The keys to making this happen were as follows:

1. I tried hard not to hog the 'chunky bits' – i.e. the exciting, challenging or enjoyable pieces of work. We broadened our knowledge and gave the team a chance to try things with clients and prospective clients – in other words, we trusted people.

2. Prior to and after the sudden change in our circumstances, the engagement of our team in the business of Landers was and remains paramount. It is our core belief that motivated, informed and above all outstanding people are the single most important factor in the success of our business. People are an asset but the right people are your greatest asset.

3. Flowing from this is the belief that we thrive by properly looking after our clients. So in the last 3 years the people who make up our team have physically grown in stature through what they do (different and more varied things than before) and how they project themselves to the clients of our business.

4. We achieved this by growing a culture of inclusion and encouraging team members to 'be their own boss', to be self-directing.

5. 'Think tanks' were set up by our non-chargeable people to see how they could help our Client Managers with certain non-chargeable work, and the business became more efficient.

6. We upped the amount of internal training, and increased the number of directly relevant courses that our team went on.

7. We took our entire team to three major practice improvement conferences and held brainstorming sessions following these so everyone plays a part in the development of the business and its future success. We encouraged them to be 'mountain people'.

   This is a concept that was explained at the conference by Frank Dick, former head of UK Athletic Coaching. In short, rather than being 'valley people' with limited horizons we encouraged a 'mountain people' outlook with a broader view and a focus on self improvement.

8. We carried on with 6 monthly career development reviews with specific goals and specific detailed follow up.

9. We carried out in-house 360 degree reviews focusing on the team and their work relationship with me, so we got parallel expectations and outcomes.

10. We all signed up to a culture of open praise, recognition and sanguine resolution of any occasional hiccups, replacing blame with a system to make sure we don't repeat mistakes.

11. We made sure that key elements of the entire team are involved directly in the recruitment of new members to ensure a cultural fit.

12. By being rigorous about recruitment, we have made sure we have got 'the right people on the bus', choosing to recruit by attitude and not qualifications. It creates a wish and willingness to help each other to find ways to solve problems and exploit opportunities. We go the extra mile for clients and each other!

13. We have a rotating chairperson across the team for the weekly WIP meeting; this gives our team full involvement on what's happening within the practice and enables them to take a leading role to make changes.

14. Because we continue to place training high on our list, we were awarded ACCA Platinum status for people development.

15. Our Investors In People (successfully re-awarded) Assessor commented, "One of the most enjoyable days he had spent with a company." He also said that he felt the "unprompted enthusiasm from the team here."

16. We continue to finish on Friday at 1.30 pm, and give our people their birthday off work.

17. Work/life balance is our primary aim. We live it, not just pay lip service.

18. We gave a non-accountant the job of organising technical people and helping them solve their time management/organisation problems. We gave people with the best skill-set a chance to shine.

19. We also encouraged our team to put themselves in the shoes of the client – and to ask the question "what are your issues?"

Success Factor 2 – Systems

Systems were always high on the agenda, but with the loss of a key member, they become even more important, and allowed the team to grow on from them. As Michael Gerber says, if you can't show me the system – it doesn't exist!

Some of the systems that are critical to our success are:

1. We have strong operational systems, both background and client facing, using AVN's System Builder software (Landers have been founder members of AVN since the year 2000) This gives certainty about qualitative aspects of the firm's output, together with making the practice more efficient internally.

2. We have a system for how to run BoardView meetings with clients which enables other team members to be confident and run these meetings without me being present. (NB: BoardView is a tremendously powerful concept whereby we earn very good recurring fees for meeting with clients regularly to help them identify, discuss and do something about the key issues facing their businesses. We regard BoardView as so crucially important to the success of our firm and our clients that we will not take on a new client unless they agree to include this in the scope of our annual contract.)

3. We use standard systems for quoting to ensure we price correctly and consistently and put it in the hands of the clients to choose what they want. This helped take the burden away from me and allowed the Client Managers to actively grow the business.

4. Our "Business Builder Forum" business club is a highly systemized process that continues to be a very good source of referrals for us. It is also an excellent way to convert prospects into clients – since it allows us to prove that we really do know about business. It enables clients and prospects to hear us talk a different language.

5. We continued with marketing and get team members to write content for press releases, with a systemised approach and systematic follow up.

Success Factor 3 – Clarity

1. We have made the practice become a game our team wants to play. We have taken the accounting disease of over-measuring out of the equation, and replaced it with clear personal expectations and financial success measures.

2. The progress towards our annual billing target (and bonus for all once we exceed the billing target) is talked through every week with everyone from the Cleaner, Client Manager and Managing Director alike.

3. We have a clear incentive strategy using a quarterly 'Pot of Gold' mini-bonus to encourage our team to look for proactive valuable work they can do for clients.

4. We are clear with clients exactly what we are going to do for them, and are transparent in our pricing. We give clients a clear "Basis of our relationship" document at the outset and we use it to live by in all our dealings with our clients. And we never bill unless it is agreed upfront.

5. We have communicated the "Basis of our relationship" document very clearly with our team so it has become an automatic part of our culture!

6. I have shared my plans and goals, as owner, with our team.

7. Most of all we have tried to be sincere and straight with each other about our expectations of one another. We have had no one leave in the last 30 months, which, if nothing else, has saved us huge amounts in recruitment fees.

My advice to other practitioners

So my advice to any practice facing similar circumstances to us... or indeed, to any practice that wants to become more successful or overcome any challenge, including the recession, is simply this...

*   Get the right people on the bus
*   Believe in systems as the answer
*   And make every message simple and clear.

Postscript

My blood pressure is 20% lower than 10 years ago, and I have never enjoyed general practice more than now with our fantastic team of truly exceptional people.

How to earn £149,400 in upfront fees in just 7 months

Back in 2007, Andrew Botham wrote to me saying that offering a One Page Plan service had added £300,000 to his firm's income.

More recently he told me that over a seven month period Mayes Business Partnership ('Mayes'), his two director practice in Accrington, had earned a further £149,400 in fees from One Page Plans. Every single penny of these fees was paid to them in full in advance. And their clients have also received two thirds of their money back from the local Business Link in the form of 'Train To Gain' funding.

One Page Plans

There are two core components to the One Page Plan service offered so successfully by Mayes and other firms:

1   A concise monthly/quarterly report in a standard "One Page Plan" format, showing a client all the key numbers that matter in their business. Crucially, this report doesn't just include the numbers that appear in a set of management accounts – it also includes all the other non financial numbers that the business considers to be really important.

2   A half day (i.e. 2-3 hour) monthly/quarterly meeting to discuss the numbers in that report in a structured and systematic way. The consequence of which is that the business makes better decisions and gets better results.

Not only is this 100% rooted in the accountancy profession's skills with numbers, it is also what many people actually expect from a good accountant. As a result, because it is such a valuable service for clients, it can also be a hugely rewarding source of recurring fees for accountants.

Earning £149,000 extra in upfront fees

Here is a step by step guide to exactly how Mayes earned their £149,000 of extra fees.

STEP 1   Make it qualify. Take your core One Page Plan service and re-label it as "Business Process Coaching." That is all Mayes had to do with their service to make it qualify for Train To Gain funding.

STEP 2   Set your pricing structure so that it works for you and your client, and also makes the most of the funding opportunity. Train To Gain funding is available to businesses with 5 or more employees. Under it, each key manager in the business can claim up to £1000 of funding for up to £1500 of One Page Plan support from the practice. The maximum funding that can be claimed by the entire management team is £7000 per business.

Mayes have always priced their One Page Planning service at £750 per meeting – and sold many of them at that full price. But Train To Gain funding means that two One Page Plan meetings worth £1500 only actually now cost the client £500. And for the many clients who can claim close to the maximum funding, it means they can get two years of quarterly One Page Plan meetings (worth £6000) for only £2000.

STEP 3   Promote the service. Start by picking up the phone and calling clients to say "You were interested in our One Page Plan service before, but the cost put you off. The good news is that now I can get you up to £7000 of funding towards it – which amounts to a two thirds discount." That type of phone call is what generated most of the £149k for Mayes.

In addition, you might want to run seminars explaining what a One Page Plan is and why it is so useful. And you should also tell your contacts about it at your next meeting with them, and in writing if you are not going to be meeting them in the near future.

Finally, also ask Business Link to refer their customers to you for the service. Mayes have found them very willing to do so, and have already earned £6000 of new fees as a result, as well as having some very exciting hot prospects in the pipeline.

STEP 4   Get payment upfront. When a client says "yes", Business Link insists that you invoice the client in full immediately, and that the client pays you in full immediately (so it is great for your cashflow). Once they have paid you, the client can then claim two thirds of the fee back from Business Link, and will generally be paid within two weeks.

STEP 5   Deliver it as normal. Mayes have made no changes to the way they deliver One Page Plans. That is because a standard One Page Plan service will automatically encompass showing (and therefore in effect "training") the management team how to:

- Set business goals, and ensure they are congruent with their personal goals

- Identify the key success drivers in the business
- Set targets for everything that matters
- Analyse and discuss actual performance
- Make better decisions
- Develop action plans for improving the business
- Implement those action plans
- Develop and improve the business
- Understand the business better
- Communicate with and lead their teams better

What if the grant situation changes?

This is exactly how it worked for Mayes in Accrington. But your Business Link may operate Train To Gain funding in a slightly different way. So you will need to find out from them how it works in your area, and then adapt the above 5 steps accordingly.

It is even possible that the grant funding may have dried up. If that happens don't give up because there is still a huge opportunity.

Remember, Mayes earned £300,000 from One Page Plans before there was any possibility of grants. So you don't need grants to make your One Page Plan service really successful.

Making tax credits work for you and your clients

Ian Rodgers, a sole practitioner trading as McGregors Business Services in Leicestershire, launched a new proactive tax credits service to meet his clients' needs more fully. As a result he earned over £6,000 in extra fees in the first month alone.

It started when Ian went on a tax credit course and realised how much scope there was to provide a better service to clients in this area. Previously, like most other firms, they had specifically excluded tax credits from the scope of their engagements. But now he realised there was a better way. So a few days later Ian launched a new four step service.

STEP 1   As his tax team work on a client's tax return, they now systematically and automatically also run the client's numbers through their tax credit software, provided one or more "triggers" are present. The triggers include, of course, having income below £58,000. It is important to note that this is not just done some of the time, when they think about it. It is part of the checklist and is done every single time. Ian estimates that in the first month of doing this with the random selection of tax returns that they have worked on, they have identified potential claims in about 15% of cases.

STEP 2   If they need more information, they get it. Then they tell the client what they have done, and what they have found. If no tax credits are available, they tell the client so and get the brownie points for at least having tried. And if they are available, they tell the client the net amount of extra cash (i.e. net of their fees) that appear to be at stake so the client can make an informed decision as to whether they want to go ahead.

STEP 3   If the client is interested, they then agree the pricing structure for the service before the work starts (so there are no surprise bills later). In the first year that involves a £395 set up fee and 10% of any extra tax credits obtained over and above what the client was receiving already. And if the client optionally wants ongoing help, extending or repeating the claim in future years, then the additional charge is £195 to £295 a year. To date every single client they have offered this to, has been happy with his fee structure – so their conversion rate from opportunity to sale has been 100%.

STEP 4   They do the work using a standard system. As a result, it can be done very professionally and very profitably by relatively junior team members.

It appears that there is a huge untapped market for tax credit support. Clients need it. And as a result, if priced and delivered properly, it can generate very significant additional fees.

The key, however, is to be proactive – i.e. not to wait until a client asks you for tax credit advice (since most never will because they have no idea of the possibilities), but to systematically identify every case where tax credits are available.

Fundamental change for a 100 year old firm

Having been established for over 100 years, you might expect this two director practice in Stockport to be rather set in its ways. Whilst this might previously have been the case, it underwent a fundamental change in 2010 that saw it:

- Win four times as many new clients as in the previous year.

- Substantially increase team morale and engagement.

- Re-ignite its desire and passion to make a difference to local businesses (including its own).

- Raise its profile to the extent that it has been asked to provide a series of 'business doctor' articles for the local press. This has established its credentials with strategic alliance partners (including two high street banks), who are now always on the lookout for new clients to introduce to McKellens.

There have been six keys to achieving all of this.

1. Engaging the team

2. Clarifying the culture

3. Getting a coach

4. Taking growth more seriously

5. Improving the lead generation systems

6. Systemising the lead conversion process

Engaging the team

Given the firm's long history and a tendency in the past not to follow through with new initiatives, there was a natural scepticism among team members when changes were proposed. The doubts were reinforced by McKellens having previously been reluctant to reveal financial figures to the team.

The decision was taken to sweep away the secrecy and involve the team more by:

- Holding monthly whole team meetings where fee targets and progress against those targets are shared

- Introducing a quarterly bonus scheme for team members with payments openly and visibly based on hitting fee targets

- Getting the team to help in making suggestions to improve client service and identifying and implementing ways to 'wow' clients

- Holding a weekly team 'huddle' on a Monday afternoon so that everyone shares what they are doing that week and where they can ask for help from other team members. This has significantly improved communication and helps each team member to understand the pressure felt by others

Added to this, the directors have:

- Clarified the firm's goals so everyone knows what it is trying to achieve and the direction in which it needs to travel

- Clearly defined the roles and responsibilities of every single person in the practice, which has brought further clarity and focus

- Increased the frequency and variety of teambuilding events. Chris Booth comments: "One of the more memorable ones was an afternoon fencing (of the epee variety); a great way to get even with the boss!"

The result of these efforts has been that team morale and engagement have increased substantially.

Clarifying the culture

Since McKellens has been around for many years and has several long-standing team members, there was a general assumption that the firm's culture and way of working were known and understood. However, nothing was defined and so a nine-point 'This is what McKellens is all about' document was produced to set out what the firm stands for, how things are done and how it treats clients and team members.

The document was produced after discussion with all team members to determine their views on the firm's current position and where it should aim to be. Because team members were involved in discussions and debate, the resulting document was a collective effort to which everyone signed up.

Chris says: "This summary of our culture is now framed and hanging up in the office for all to see, including visitors. And it has a profound impact, since by clarifying the standards we work by it has actually helped to improve those standards, and ensure that we all operate to them."

Using a business coach

Right at the very start of the process, they engaged a business coach to help define where the firm wanted to be and get the team involved. The next task was to create the time to be able to plan and implement the necessary changes in the business. To achieve this, the business coach:

- Provided an external source of ideas and questioning of why things were done in the way they previously were. This enabled team members, and particularly the directors to focus on the essentials and to ignore trivial items. In particular, the coach's marketing expertise helped the practice move forward much more quickly and effectively.

- Ensured that far more of the "talk" actually turned into action.

Chris comments: "Getting a coach is by far the best investment we have made! Seriously, get someone from outside to hold you to account for the things you know that need to be done."

Taking growth more seriously

Historically there had been no formal growth strategy for the business. This was corrected by:

- Setting a target of growing the fee income of the firm by 10% for each of the next ten years. Chris says: "We could have aimed for more, but felt that 10% was a manageable and achievable growth rate. It would allow us to concentrate on winning high quality new clients and still achieve compound growth of more than 150% over 10 years."

- Focusing on new client acquisition, especially on winning better quality clients with a higher value of annual fees.

- Concentrating on proactively identifying additional work with the existing client base in order to increase the average fee per client.

- Creating a One Page Plan to keep focused on the key numbers of the business.

Improving lead generation systems

To achieve the planned growth, it was necessary to generate more leads from within and beyond the client base. To do this, the firm:

- Joined the B4B networking organisation, which has been a very fruitful source of introductions.

- Worked with the local Chamber of Commerce and used the BBF seminar resources from AVN to deliver a core syllabus of seventeen business improvement sessions to twenty local businesses under the Business Growth Forum identity. This has produced a 50% conversion rate of businesses attending the forum.

- Also used the BBF resources to launch a new series of McKellens Business Accelerator seminars.

- Ran a hugely successful "How to get an extra £2 million" seminar, sponsored by the Royal Bank of Scotland, with 72 attendees.

- Introduced clients to the idea of having regular BoardView meetings where their One Page Plan is discussed.

- Developed a culture of abundance and saying 'thank you' to clients, contacts and introducers. For example taking clients on a series of guided mountain walks in the Lake District, which also provided a networking opportunity.

Chris says: "The seminars and events have helped us increase our average fee value and led to a good number of small businesses buying our quarterly *BoardView* and *One Page Plan* services. And the other initiatives have brought us a strong stream of referrals and leads."

Systemising the lead conversion process

Generating leads is only the first part of the challenge, and so McKellens also set up a process that would enable it to convert a higher proportion of those leads into new clients. This involves:

- Sending a handwritten 'thank you' note and gift to whoever made the referral

- Undertaking background research by obtaining information from the web (including from the company website, Facebook page and LinkedIn profiles), a CreditSafe report, details from the referrer and prior year accounts, if available

- Making an initial telephone call to establish what is required, to obtain copies of the last full accounts and management accounts, and to tell them about the pre-meeting questionnaire they will receive

- Sending an information pack that contains a questionnaire designed to determine what the prospective client wants and to identify their views of the business, a biography of McKellens, testimonials from clients and leaflets on the firm's benchmarking, financial performance review and One Page business plan services

- Producing a benchmarking report using the information on the accounts and questionnaire

- Making a further telephone call to clarify the needs of the prospective client and prepare for the meeting by establishing their general positioning, business goals, personal goals and business challenges

- Conducting a first meeting where:

- The prospect is given a copy of the benchmarking report and a "The Numbers" folder that contains a complete Performance Measurement and Improvement system

- They are shown how these documents, and the other things McKellens can do for them, will help them to improve the key numbers in their business, including sales, profits, cashflow and their capital value

- Times Up pricing software is used live to iteratively calculate as many different fixed fee quotations as is necessary to find the combination of price and package that is perfect for the client

- And when they sign up, sending them a handwritten 'thank you' card to welcome them as a client, along with a welcome pack and a welcome gift (typically either a copy of the book "Beat the Recession" business book, a copy of the "Simple Stuff That Works" interactive profit improvement software or a branded memory stick).

Chris explains: "Probably our most successful strategy has been to create this really carefully thought through sales conversion system, document it, and then make sure that it is used consistently every time we meet a prospect. That sort of discipline and attention to detail has really paid dividends. It makes our meetings far more professional and impressive. And that in turn means that a far higher percentage of prospects say 'yes'. In addition, having a system to follow also makes our job much easier, since we don't have to keep reinventing the wheel."

Sole practitioner grows by 38% by no longer personally doing compliance work

Meades & Co, which is run by sole practitioner Paul Meades, is a Watford based practice that, in the last two years, has:

- Strategically reduced its client base from 650 to 390

- Increased turnover by 38%, partly by making itself more attractive to better quality clients, and partly by providing a better service to its existing high quality clients

- Reduced debtors from £80,000 to £20,000 by using fixed price agreements and direct debits

- Replaced its £40,000 overdraft with a very healthy credit balance

Employ someone else to do your work

Paul explains: "I used to have lots of ideas for improving the business, but never had the time to really turn them into action. It was really frustrating.

So I decided that the only way to break out of that vicious circle was to invest some money in employing a really good fully qualified accountant, and then pass all my clients and compliance work over to her."

"After all, every entrepreneur knows that you have to speculate to accumulate, and invest in order to earn a return. And that single decision has been the catalyst for all the good things that have happened to us since."

Invest the time saved in developing your business

Instead of being bogged down with compliance work, Paul now spends his time thinking about his business as a business, working out how to improve it, and making sure that his improvement plans actually get implemented.

In particular he has:

- Identified the types of ideal clients he wants his practice to be built around (those with turnover between £500,000 and £10 million and with 5 or more employees)

- Focused on understanding what those ideal clients really want and need, and redesigned his service offerings around those wants and needs

- Graded his current clients, and deliberately exited those for whom the new look firm was no longer really suitable

- Studied the research about the kind of pricing that clients prefer and that works best for firms. This has led to him use fixed price agreements, usually paid in advance by direct debit. "If a prospect does not want to pay in this way, we part company, which we have found to be an excellent way of filtering and focusing our energies on the right clients," explains Paul. He also uses value billing where possible, such as with tax planning.

- Been much more proactive with clients, particularly around tax planning and general business advice

"At the moment I am still working long hours and very hard. But I know that it is just a short term situation while I lay the essential foundations for our success. And anyway, it is so much more satisfying working hard on these kind of things than it ever was slaving over yet another accounts file, since I know that this is really moving my business and my life forwards."

Serve clients better

In order to serve clients better and more proactively, Paul has also introduced a number of new systems, including:

- **Improving turnaround times** – They now use their IRIS Practice Management software to measure turnaround times on all jobs, with a red flag system for those that are "late" compared to a demanding target deadline. These measures, which are reported on the firm's One Page Plan, have led to a "dramatic improvement in turnaround times as the entire team has been made accountable for on time delivery."

- **Quarterly phone calls** – They also use IRIS Practice Management to trigger proactive telephone calls to clients at least every three months. Essentially these are "how are things going?" calls. But they use a system developed by Paul, based on four key questions: Can we help you to grow your business? Can we help you to increase the value of your business? Can we help you to improve your personal wealth? And can we help you to save tax? "Clients really value us taking an interest in this way, and often it results in them asking us to do some extra work for them," says Paul.

- **Colour coded files** – "Having graded clients, we use different colour files for the As, Bs and Cs, since it's a great visual reminder of who is who. Every client gets excellent service of course. But the colour coding makes it easier for us to prioritise the order that we do things, and also to identify where it is most appropriate to go even further than normal to delight a client."

- **Advanced tax planning** – "Tax is such a key area for clients that, through our membership of a network, we have formed arrangements with many of the UK's leading advanced tax planning specialists. Under those arrangements, they do all the technical work, and carry all the engagement risk, and they give us a share of the fees they charge to the client in the form of a payaway. In addition, we usually charge the tax payer an extra fee for 'holding their hands' during the process. Although we often reward our existing clients, by charging them a lower extra fee than we would charge to someone who just wanted help with tax planning, without otherwise being a client."

Proactive marketing email marketing

Having transformed the practice into something that meets the needs of its clients superbly well, the final piece of the jigsaw was to become much better at proactively marketing themselves to their ideal prospects.

"One of the most effective ways we do that," explains Paul, "is by sending out an email every two weeks containing business tips we glean from books, articles and seminars. And because of the email software we use, we are able to track which of the recipients (clients, prospects and bank managers) open the email and which articles they read. So we proactively follow up by systematically contacting them along the lines of 'We see you were interested in our article on...' and use the resulting conversation to add value."

"It's proving to be a really good way to build relationships and develop a dialogue. And that in turn is also proving very worthwhile commercially. For example, only yesterday it led a prospect to sign up for our BoardView service at £500 per session, without even switching their accounts work to us."

Other proactive marketing

"We are also achieving great results from our BBF business club in a way that was totally unexpected. We organised our first BBF meeting around the concept of attracting prospects to find out more about us, but didn't expect that the attendees would view the BBF as a great way to network and share insights, ideas and business tips with each other."

"So, rather than us having to do formal presentations at club meetings, we are now mainly facilitators for sessions at which our clients and prospects decide what they want to discuss together, and in the process they discover how we can help them to improve their businesses or solve the issues they have. It has kind of taken on a life of its own and is growing in numbers rapidly which is, of course, raising our profile and attracting even more clients to us. Because of this we are now also starting to be asked to be guest speakers at other people's events, which is also helping us to gain new clients of the right type. As a result, everybody wins! "

"Obviously, launching a raft of proactive marketing initiatives takes time and effort so, even though we are a small firm, I took the decision that the time had come to employ a full time marketing coordinator, and what a great move that has turned out to be."

"For example, our BBF's are now organised in-house by the team, which frees up even more of my time. And having a full time focus means that our social media marketing has also really taken off, to the point where we have business gurus such as Robert Craven following us on Twitter and KPMG thanking us for our tweets! We have even been able to start using LinkedIn to gain new clients because of our connections to their contacts."

Taking massive action

'Taking massive action' was this practice's solution to the challenge of becoming more commercial and improving the business. This was partly born out of a realisation that most accountants are now becoming more proactive and it needed to differentiate itself somehow from the rest within the local area.

Becoming an expert in its field

Murray Associates is a small practice in Paisley, Scotland, with one Director and just four team members. Despite its small size, it set out to be seen as an expert in the field of helping clients understand what drives their success, measure those drivers, and use the insights gained to create action plans to help clients improve their growth, profits, cashflow and other key results.

One way it sought to achieve this was by running regular seminars. This started with an anti-recession seminar that was staged in response to the needs of clients, and other contacts, who were worried by the economic situation and were looking for help.

From small beginnings, the seminars grew to a series of regular events, with the practice now running six "Business Growth Club" seminars a year at two different locations, plus other one-off seminars on business topics of interest to clients and prospects. The growing popularity and reputation of the seminars led to an increased demand for them to give additional talks. As a result, last year they had eight external speaking engagements in addition to the 18 organised by the practice itself. And each of these 26 platforms added to their reputation and contacts list.

Murray Associates' Director Gloria Murray says: "We also run stand-alone seminars with key introducers, such as banks, Regus offices, Aberdeen Businesswoman's Network and Renfrewshire Chamber of Commerce. I've been asked to run seminars at Business Growth clubs throughout Central Scotland, which are run by the regeneration agencies. One of these even resulted in us producing our very own DVD on "Pricing for Maximum Profit", which we now give to contacts and clients."

Gloria added, "None of this would have been possible if our seminar programme had consisted of tax updates and other equally worthy but dull subjects. Instead, our seminars are based on things that entrepreneurs really want to come and listen to, such as how to increase sales, how to price more profitably, how to get paid on time, getting the best from your team and running a more efficient and profitable business. And it is that focus that has been the key to our success."

How it all helps businesses

The Business Growth Club seminars evolved from the original Business Builder Forum format and are intended to help the practice's clients gain access to business growth at a fraction of the price of traditional business consultancy.

One client who benefitted from her attendance at the seminars is Ruth McIntosh of RDF Design. Ruth is a graphic designer who was in her third year in business but was working long hours for little reward and struggling with her cash flow and profitability.

Since becoming involved in the Murray Associates Business Growth Club seminars she has transformed her business in many ways:

- She has changed her terms and conditions so that she is now paid monthly when working on a project. Payments were previously dependent on stages being reached, which could be delayed by the client not moving things on. This has vastly improved her cash flow.

- She has developed work packages that give her clients a much better understanding of the amount of work involved – and as a result the prices she has been able to command have typically increased by 50%.

- The seminars have given her a much better understanding of the importance of measuring everything that matters to her in her business. And that in turn has helped her to get better results by making better decisions.

- She has seen an increase in her profit of 1019% in the past year.

Ruth comments: "I joined the Murray Associates' Business Growth Club after being impressed by the positive approach of Gloria's talk at their anti-recession seminar. They really provide a hands-on approach to helping you develop your business through understanding those important figures."

"Through the ongoing support of the Business Growth Club (whose members have become my 'business family') and latterly a one-on-one Business Potential Review, I have a better understanding of how to develop my business so that it is not only successful but also profitable."

"Gloria and Gerry are fantastic to work with and take a non jargon approach to helping you understand your finances. They have a real passion for helping businesses succeed, bringing a breath of fresh air to business development training."

Publicity though public speaking

A major benefit of running the various seminars and being invited to external events, is the publicity that this brings. The name of Murray Associates has become well known and is now widely recognised when the practice undertakes speaking engagements and attends other networking events.

"Many people have already heard of us and assume we are a very large firm," remarks Gloria. "Of course, we don't try to deceive them so we tell them our size. Instead, we play on our small team by accentuating the positives – knowing our clients personally, being able to offer a great personal service, the quality of what we provide and being accessible."

The seminars continually add to Murray Associates' reputation and bring it into contact with many potential clients, increasing its prospects for future growth. In fact, Gloria reckons the practice now has around 400 'warm contacts' who have become part of its networking group, advocates, referrers or clients. So the future looks very bright for them.

According to Gloria: "Seminars have been a great way of generating leads. We believe it is essential to develop relationships with potential clients and have found leads become warmer the more they have contact with us. It can be a longer term game but we want to be seen as expert accountants and business growth specialists, not as excellent salespeople."

Improving other service areas

Seminars, of course, are by no means the only thing Murray Associates has done: it has also put a lot of effort into improving the service it offers in other areas. For example, in addition to helping its clients have a better business and make more money, it also specialises in helping them to pay less tax. Some of the keys to its success in these other areas have included tax planning and customer service.

They systematically carry out a detailed review to identify the most appropriate tax planning opportunities for every client including:

- For example, with sole traders and partnerships they will use Incorporation Tax Planner software to produce a preliminary estimate of the tax savings from incorporation (with and without goodwill capitalisation), and will extrapolate the savings over a number of years to give clients a better feel for what is really at stake.

- For companies they use Remuneration Tax Planner software to show clients how much tax they will save by using the most efficient combination of salary, bonus, dividends and interest on loan accounts, as well as more advanced options such as EBTs and EFRBS when they were available.

- Unlike many accountants, they also take tax credits fully into account – ensuring that the combined impact on the client's tax and tax credits position is always considered. And by building tax credits expertise within the practice they can also help clients to claim more tax credits than ever before.

They systematically improve the business experience for their clients including:

- A particular focus on improving the existing customer service now guaranteeing a 30-day turnaround on accounts.

- All work also carries a no quibble, 100% money back guarantee.

- There is now a rolling programme of contact with clients, including a telephone survey. Contacting clients more regularly ensures the practice has more information about what is happening in their business and can offer them timely support. In the current climate, it has become more important than ever to ensure that the clients feel supported. Gloria says, "We find out how they are feeling and discover what else we can offer them."

Gloria believes that the results and comments received from the surveys have been extremely useful for the practice. "We follow up on every one with the actions we are taking as a result of their feedback. This ensures clients know we are listening to them. It has also meant we have packaged some of our services differently since we've been able to identify our clients' needs and wants much better. In particular, we realised that small limited companies, especially the ones with few employees, struggle with the complexities of a limited company. We now have a particular package that does everything our clients told us they wanted."

Getting control of work and cash flow

Another one of the firm's focuses over the last few years has been to systemise more of its key working practices in order to drive out inefficiencies, drive down costs and turnaround times, and improve the service experience for clients.

These improved systems mean that more work is now done on time, or even early, as Gloria confirms: "We have a system in place so around 95% of the January deadline work is done by September of the previous year. This means we are less stressed coming up to the 'busy' months and we can look for opportunities that other accountants in the area can't fulfil. We have spare capacity that we can use to our advantage. We do more tax planning as we're not fire fighting at the end of the year using out of date information."

Through increased contact with potential clients and systems improvements, turnover has already increased by 10% without any need to increase the size of the team. And more growth is confidently expected.

The practice has also tightened up on credit control and now collects 40% of its fee income by direct debit. All new clients are required to pay by this method and existing clients are being converted gradually. The result is that debtor days now average only four and were down to 1.8 days at one point.

Modern methods of marketing

Social networking is now an integral part of Murray Associates' marketing strategy. Gloria explains: "We want to attract younger clients before the old ones retire so we have to use the networks younger clients are using. If you are still doing business in the old ways, you are missing out on a lot of young dynamic businesses."

This move to more modern methods has also led to a degree of rebranding since the firm's previous logo was thought not to match its current image. As a result Murray Associates employed the services of Ruth at RDF Design, whom they previously met through the Business Growth Club. She developed a new business image which now features in all of the promotional material and the website and this has helped to improve the impact of Murray Associates with these new target markets.

The bottom line

Despite the 'massive action' that has been required to expand the practice's contacts and services, Gloria is convinced it has all been worthwhile.

"We have expanded our network of contacts rapidly and our team is less stressed, ensuring a better working environment. We are able to capitalise on opportunities that are now coming our way, whereas before we would not have been able to take time to develop new clients or projects. So we are now really well placed for sustained future success."

A systematic approach to incorporations

Peterborough based Nino Pucacco of P&A Accountancy Services wrote this about how he earned an extra £28,250 from the first four clients he talked to about incorporating...

"I would not have believed this possible at any time, let alone in the jaws of a recession... but in the last three months we have proactively and systematically talked to four of our smallish clients and as a result they have agreed to pay us an extra £28,250 in fees to help them incorporate. Those are quite big fees for us since we are a small two partner firm with three staff."

In all four cases they were unincorporated businesses that were all paying us £1,200-£1,800 pa for their annual accounting service, and one of them was also buying management accounts from us. So they are very typical clients, and yet the extra fees we have earned amount to more than four times our core GRF from these clients.

In all four cases we had previously talked to them about incorporation, but they had never really been interested. So this time we decided to tackle the whole process differently. Here is a step by step summary of exactly what we did that worked so well:

STEP 1   **A three meeting plan**

We mapped out a three meeting approach – since clearly the issues were too big for the client take in properly at just one meeting. The first meeting was to sow the seed. The second meeting was to add the detail and obtain a cheque from the client for £299 + VAT to cover the cost of an independent business valuation. And the third meeting was for the client and, crucially, their significant other, to come in to discuss the valuation and have all their remaining questions answered.

Clearly all of this involved proactively investing time with our clients that we had no certainty of ever being paid for – since the fee was only agreed after the third meeting. But it was unquestionably the right thing to do for our clients, and because profits are a consequence of doing right things for clients, it was clearly also the right thing to do for our practice.

Seeing clients in the right order

We identified the first four clients we were going to talk to, and the order in which we would approach them. Getting the order right was essential, since we wanted to fine tune our process and our skills with the simpler cases before moving on to the more demanding ones. This was also reflected in the fees we were able to earn, which were (in chronological order) £750, £2,500, £4,000 and £21,000.

Making the benefits crystal clear

Across our three meetings we diligently went through all the pros and cons of incorporation, as of course you must. But once we got to the tax issue we found it invaluable to use Incorporation Tax Planner software to be able to instantly show the client the tax position with and without incorporation, and to do "what if" calculations to see how robust the tax savings were.

In most cases, however, the clincher was the tax saving from capitalising goodwill and creating a loan account balance that the client could subsequently draw down on free of tax. The software we used allowed us to both instantly quantify the tax savings, and also to show them how big their resulting tax free loan account balance would be. And it was this latter number that proved decisive for most of our clients.

Pricing properly

As we went into this process, we were acutely aware of two pieces of research. Firstly, most accountants grossly under-price incorporation services – and as a result are forced to cut corners and not provide the comprehensive service that clients really need. Secondly, research shows that, despite what their accounts show, most accountants actually make a loss. In my opinion those two facts are inextricably linked: when you charge too little you let your clients down by not being able to do a proper job, and you let yourself down by making losses.

We didn't want to let anybody down, so we decided to use value pricing by linking the fee to the amount of tax saved. This was made easier for us because our incorporation software automatically calculates a value based fee on the screen. What is more, because the fee is calculated by the computer you tend to meet much less price resistance than you would if the client felt you had just conjured it up out of thin air yourself.

As a result, we have significantly enriched our clients' financial affairs. To our clients, therefore, our fees represent only a tiny fraction of the extra tax they are saving, so from their point of view they are getting a really good deal. And from our point of view we are being paid properly and profitably for our contribution. So everybody wins.

Final thoughts

The extra £28,250 we have earned from the above is just the start for us. Obviously we have other unincorporated clients to talk to as well. But we are finding that, across, the board, being more systematically proactive than ever before is creating a mountain of extra work (and profitable extra fees) for us. So much for the recession!"

Nino added this further comment in early 2011

"To bring you up to date, during 2009-2010 we generated a total of £45,000 in additional fees from nine incorporations. But I cannot stress highly enough the importance of charging the right fee to do a thorough job for the client, and of getting an independent valuation. All of our goodwill valuations were challenged by HMRC, but because there were sufficient fees to cover the additional time required, we were able to spend the correct amount of time to defend each case. That, coupled with the fact that we had already obtained independent valuations, has meant that to date every single valuation has been successfully defended."

Better service, better profits and a better quality of life

This small practice, based in Chertsey, has used the recession as an opportunity to carry out a fundamental restructuring and reorganisation of its clients, team and working practices.

As a result, it is now much leaner and much better prepared for what the recovery has to offer. Profits and cashflow are substantially better. And, for those involved, work is now much more enjoyable and a whole lot less stressful.

Concentrating on the ideal client

The first major step the firm took was to grade its clients to identify those that met its ideal client criteria. And, as a result, a large proportion of its client base (i.e. those which didn't meet the criteria) were sold off. The main aim of the exercise, as Managing Director Nick Robinson points out, was to be able to "get closer to the clients that matter and get rid of the clients that don't."

The reduced workload meant that the team of six could be trimmed to two i.e. Nick and a practice manager, who is also Nick's wife. But, as Nick explains: "The redundancies were not as a result of the recession but as a result of needing a work/life balance change, but it has definitely helped!"

The change to work/life balance was quite startling, with Nick's personal working hours reduced by around one third. Instead of sometimes having to start work at 4am and often not finishing until 7 or 8pm, working hours are now a regular and more acceptable 8am to 5pm from Monday to Friday. This has led to a far better working environment and a greatly improved social life for Nick.

"We no longer work on Saturdays and have more time to pursue personal hobbies and activities," remarks Nick. "I've also been able to take days off and play golf with clients."

Improving service with fewer people

Reducing team numbers and hours has not led to a lower level of service for clients. In fact, quite the opposite is the case, as Nick confirms: "Being able to spend more time with fewer clients is working well in these recessionary times, as they feel I am taking a more active interest in their business."

Robinson Brothers has made strenuous efforts to help its clients through the difficult economic times. These efforts include providing specific additional services such as:

- Giving out copies of the book "Beat The Recession"

- Including an anti recession toolkit in the end of year recommendations report given to every client

- Working closer with certain clients on specific subjects such as management accounts, product profitability analysis and alternative finance arrangements

- Undertaking an internal management role with one client to help develop the business during the recession.

Power in Numbers

As part of this re-organisation and new focus the firm has also rebranded itself, replacing the traditional sounding Robinson Brothers name with the much more modern "Power in Numbers." They also launched a distinctive new website to reinforce the message that they have changed and are now different to many other accountants. And it is a refreshingly honest website:

What Nick says on his website homepage

"The first thing you should know is that I've run the practice with my wife, Susan, since 1988. So we've lots of experience. What we don't have is lots of clients. And that's deliberate. In 2008, we restructured our business so that we could focus on working only with the clients that were serious about their businesses, i.e. we became more dedicated to them.

Commercial suicide? Far from it. We choose our clients very carefully. We like them and they seem to like the plain-talking, straight-forward business sense we offer them. Of course, any new clients have to pass the same selection criteria as our old clients.

Getting the balance right between work and home life is vital at any time, but when you're in business together, as Susan and I are, it's doubly important.

Don't get me wrong... we love the work we do and helping our clients is always our biggest priority. And if there's a panic, we'll be there to help out. But we now recognise that we are in charge of our own lives and plan our time accordingly.

Not having many clients gives us another advantage over most of the other firms – we have time to talk to you more often... to find out how your business is doing and understand what really makes it tick. After all, if we don't know the fundamentals of your business, how can we help? And that's why we have regular meetings and discussions with our clients.

It also means if you call to speak to us, you'll get straight through."

Better planning means better efficiency and profits

"With our new streamlined business it was easier than ever before to budget our annual working hours, and the related income from the reduced client base. And this in turn led to a boost in overall efficiency through better planning and organisation" explained Nick. "The outcome is that jobs now go through with fewer interruptions and job turnaround time has improved from an average of 25 days down to 12 days."

Efforts have also been made to improve cash flow and revenue, with all billing being done in advance and most clients paying by direct debit. Fixed price agreements are renewed much more quickly than before and credit control has been tightened. The result is that cash flow is almost 30% better than previously.

Overall, team costs have been reduced by £8,000 a month and profitability is up by £22,000.

Creating a more enjoyable business

Nick has no doubts that the drastic efforts to reshape the business have been a resounding success: "The company is far more enjoyable to run, more efficient, more profitable, more proactive and provides a better service to customers, making them feel better during these difficult times."

Equally, he is quite certain about the key factors in making the practice a success in difficult economic times. He summarises them as: "Being proactive. Focus on the most important clients and build protective walls around them. Provide them with the little 'wow' factors that really make a difference. Keep in constant contact, even if you are just 'touching base' with them."

The service secrets taking a firm to £1 million

In September 2007, Lincoln-based sole practitioner Russell Payne and his team of 16 decided to make an Olympic bid. Not to host the Olympics, of course, but to become a £1m firm by the time the Olympics started. That was a brave target since their turnover at the time was just over £400,000. By mid 2010 they were on track, with turnover having grown to £723,000. And by March 2011 they were at £826,000.

Russell and his team are passionate about providing the best possible service. And for them that means aiming to continually exceed (not just "meet" or "satisfy") expectations, taking the time to really listen to clients, proactively and continually coming up with ideas to help them grow and improve their profits, and proactively identifying their clients' issues, problems and opportunities and providing timely recommendations and solutions.

Two examples of how they do this are the way they provide great service through their Bootcamp programme, and how they leave nothing to chance by regularly measuring their service performance using a simple but powerful "Traffic Light" system.

Giving great service through "Bootcamps"

The practice runs regular one day "Bootcamp your business" workshops for local businesses. These free sessions, presented by Russell himself, are designed to help local businesses become more successful and profitable. Regularly attracting 40 entrepreneurs a time, these workshops not only cement his relationships with existing clients, but typically they help him win new clients every time he runs them.

Spurred on by the success of his original Bootcamps, Russell has also started running various other mini bootcamps, eg Website and Social Media workshops, presented by one of Russell's joint venture partners with expertise in those areas.

According to Russell: "The key to great service is to really work out what clients want and need – and help them to get it. And when you do that your practice will grow like wildfire – since not only do clients stay loyal, but they also buy lots of additional services from you and they tell other people how good you are. So before long you have a really powerful referral engine working flat out to drive you on to greater success."

"Our seminar programme is a really important part of this since it leverages our time, delivers the ideas and support that clients really need (the same ideas and support that most accountants run a mile from!), and gives non clients an easy way to feel the quality before they start to work with us."

Using traffic lights to check that their service really is great

Most firms are afraid to ask their clients to rate their service – presumably because they are frightened of what they may hear! But not at Russell Payne & Co. Every month the firm sends every client a simple Traffic Light style email that asks them to click on one of three traffic light colours:

- **Red** means "I have a problem and there is something I would like to talk to you about straight away"

- **Amber** means "I have a minor issue with your service and would appreciate a call"

- **Green** means "I am happy and no current issues, but thanks for asking anyway"

Not only have they invested in developing the technology to automate the process of sending out the emails and instantly processing the replies (www. trafficlightfeedback.co.uk). But they have also invested time and money in creating a watertight system for ensuring that every single amber and red reply is followed up in a timely fashion. And they then report all of the key findings to the entire team every month, so that everyone understands the reality of their current service performance and is continuously focused on making it better and better.

As Russell explains: "There are so many advantages to measuring service performance in this way. Firstly, since it only takes a few seconds for anyone to respond, a very high proportion of clients do actually respond, which was rarely the case with the other feedback systems we've tried."

"Secondly, where a client is unhappy it gives us the chance to nip things in the bud before they get out of hand. Thirdly, quite often the process gets clients talking to us about additional services that they go on to buy from us. So it not only helps us to keep clients, but it also helps us to earn bigger fees from them."

"And finally, it gives us an objective yardstick to measure ourselves against, which in turn means we are able to continually challenge ourselves to provide even better service."

A systemised approach to inheritance tax planning

Stephen Docherty is a sole practitioner in Glasgow who is currently getting 26% of his clients signing up for his new £750 Inheritance Tax Healthcheck service. He explains: "Over the years we have often talked to clients about IHT planning, but it has always been difficult to make the most of this. Now though, we finally seem to have found a methodology that works."

That methodology consists of the following six steps:

STEP 1   They bought an off-the-shelf IHT healthcheck system. "Even though we had to change it a little, for example, so that the wording in the standard letters fitted our style, getting a ready to use solution saved us an enormous amount of time and prevented us having to reinvent the wheel."

STEP 2   They appointed one of their qualified team members, Carol, to run the system. "Having one person really focus on it meant that, even though she is a generalist rather than a tax specialist, she has very rapidly got fully up to speed on the key IHT planning issues and opportunities. So she is getting real job satisfaction and we are benefitting from substantial economies of scale and effort."

STEP 3   Initially they identified a first tranche of 19 clients for whom they thought IHT planning was an issue that needed addressing. So they sent those 19 a letter from the system offering an IHT Healthcheck for £750. "They were mostly people we had talked to about IHT in the past, but never managed to follow through with. And even without us doing any kind of follow up at all, five of them replied to the letter saying that they wanted us to do the Healthcheck for them. So that was a 26% take up rate on the first batch of clients we wrote to."

Essentially the letter said the following:

> People generally think of Inheritance Tax as a tax on the "rich", however increasing numbers are being caught in its net.
>
> Using our knowledge of your financial background we believe that we may be able to help you and that you could benefit from our Inheritance Tax Planning service.
>
> Our service has been designed to give you complete peace of mind that your wishes will be respected, your loved ones will get more money, and everything will be made as easy as possible for your family.
>
> In order to achieve this, we will conduct an Inheritance Health Check and report to you with our recommendations for a fixed fee of £750 plus VAT. This will include advising you what we think you should do, and how much Inheritance Tax you can save by doing it.
>
> Where our Initial Health Check recommends a more comprehensive tax planning approach, we will provide you with a quote in advance of implementing that support.

STEP 4   Next they used the flexible report template in the system to quickly and easily create a high impact 10-15 page personalised report, giving a plain English explanation of the client's exposure to IHT, and making suggestions and recommendations for how they can mitigate that exposure.

STEP 5   The report is then presented and talked through at a meeting.

STEP 6   Where the client wants to implement any of the recommendations in the report, the firm quotes a separate and additional implementation fee for the extra work involved. "The initial £750 fee covers the Healthcheck, report and meeting. Although in some cases we reduced it slightly to reflect the fact that some of the groundwork had been covered by previous IHT discussions with them. But that is just the start. Once you've quantified the size of their potential IHT bills, and set out their options, most clients will ask you to help them actually do some planning. So that means extra fees for extra work, covering anything from annual fees for producing detailed personal balance sheets, to setting up trusts and doing whatever else it takes."

According to Stephen: "Because we use a proven system to do all of this it typically takes about 4-5 hours of time (much of which is non partner time) to produce the report and meet the client to discuss it. So at a fee of £750 that is profitable work for us. Much more importantly, though, it is hugely valuable to clients. So everybody wins."

He added, "Obviously the next step for us is to roll out exactly the same process to the rest of our client base. Since that way we can make an even bigger difference to even more of our clients – and in the process be very well rewarded ourselves."

Nine ways to start where other accountants finish

Sobell Rhodes is a long established and still rapidly growing 6-partner firm, based in Pinner and the West End of London, that was recently named as the Accountancy Age Medium Size Firm of The Year and as 2020's Most Innovative Large Accountancy Firm.

Its mission is to "start where other accountants finish." And this includes its own performance metrics, since benchmarking analysis suggests that its client satisfaction scores are near the top of the scale and, as a consequence, so too are its profits per partner.

In no particular order, here are just some of the innovative things they do that have helped to make the firm so successful:

1. **Client of the month award** – Once a month team members are asked to nominate the client that they have most enjoyed working with, and the reasons why. All team members then vote for the "Client of the Month", who then receives a mahogany and brass plaque as an expression of the firm's gratitude and appreciation.

2. **Free consultations for family members** – All family members of clients are entitled to a free consultation with the firm, worth up to £100, to help them with any tax, financial or accounting issue that they may have. As well as being good service, this offer also provides a source of potential new clients for the firm.

3. **Free business improvement input** – Clients and contacts are invited to free seminars and workshops on business improvement topics such as Beat the Recession, Improve your Profits, and Strategic Planning. They are also sent a bi-monthly e-mail that focuses on ideas for helping small and medium sized business become more successful.

4. **Commitment to BNI** – Long term membership of three major BNI chapters and a reputation for living the BNI philosophy of "Givers Gain", has created over £2.7 million of extra business for Sobell Rhodes. In the last year alone, BNI referrals have resulted in additional fees for the firm of £440k.

5. **Written Referral and Service Agreements** – Formalising reciprocal referral arrangements with third parties outside BNI, who share the firm's values, culture, and commitment to service excellence, typically creates more than £100,000 in fees a year for the firm.

6. **The Sobell Rhodes Referral Exchange** – This is a new initiative designed to introduce clients to each other and to new business opportunities. Unsurprisingly it has been very well received by clients who really value Sobell Rhodes' commitment to helping them get new customers.

7. **The Professional Property Circle** – This is a group founded by Sobell Rhodes and made up of approximately 10 professional firms specialising in the property sector. The group meets once a month over breakfast with the aim of both reciprocal referrals and providing multi-disciplinary property advice. It has been an excellent source of new property clients for the firm.

8. **"Proactive Package"** – All new clients are offered a package of support to bring them up to the level of the firm's existing clients so that they are better placed to weather the recessionary storm. This package includes:

    *   The 1-Hour Business Energiser – to identify the needs and wants of the business owners and management teams.

    *   Cash Flow Review – to make sure they are making the most of all available opportunities to improve debt collection and cash flow.

    *   A Wealth Building Review – to make sure that their investments, pensions, mortgages, life and health insurances are optimised to protect them and their family as well as maximising the opportunities for increasing their future personal wealth.

    *   A Computer Systems Review – including a full IT review and up to £2,000 worth of leading business software free-of-charge, including Sage 50, QuickBooks, Business Plan Pro, Marketing Plan Pro and other software applications.

    *   A Finance Options Review – to make sure that their plans are financed in the most effective way possible.

9. **Making preliminary recommendations without charging** – The firm is acutely aware of two major research findings. Firstly, that clients want their accountants to be more proactive. And secondly, that clients hate surprise bills. So Sobell Rhodes now systematically looks for ways to make preliminary recommendations to clients (i.e. recommendations that can help the client save tax, improve cashflow or in some other way solve a problem or make the most of an opportunity) without charging for those preliminary recommendations.

What they have found is that, if their preliminary recommendations are good, clients will do one of two things: either say thank you, or say "that's interesting, can you help me implement that idea?" The former is a good result. But the latter is even better, since the client is actually asking to buy some further help, and all the practice has to do is agree the price and terms for doing that extra work.

One of the specific ways they make these preliminary recommendations is by automatically producing a Benchmarking report and a Key Improvement Possibilities report for each client, and discussing these at the annual accounts finalisation meeting. The latter report usually covers a range of ideas and related preliminary recommendations to:

- improve profits and cash flow based on the benchmarking findings
- save tax
- protect family assets and wealth
- improve personal wealth
- structure borrowings more efficiently, and
- plan for eventual exit, and perhaps also retirement

50% annual growth made possible by outsourcing

This small practice in West Byfleet, Surrey, with a principal and six team members, has increased its GRF by 50% and transformed its cashflow and profitability over the last twelve months. And it has largely achieved this by outsourcing some of its core accounts work, so it can concentrate on developing and improving other key areas of the business.

Outsourcing work creates time for more important tasks

Although some of the team were initially sceptical about the effectiveness of outsourcing, it has produced some significant benefits for the practice:

- Giving them the ability to increase their client base at a rapid rate, secure in the knowledge that they have the resources to properly deliver all the resulting work.

- Taking the pressure off 'doing' the work has created more time to improve client service.

- The team members have also been freed-up to take more responsibility in nurturing client relationships and being more proactive with clients. This has not only aided their personal development but also given them a much more enjoyable, interesting and rewarding workload.

They have also been able to use the time freed-up to evaluate and implement new ideas, systems and tools to improve the practice further. And some of the key improvements this has led to are described below.

Making visitors feel special

A new system was introduced to improve the experience of people visiting the office. Principal Joe Sole explains how it works: "When a meeting is arranged at our office with a client or prospect, an invitation is sent by email. Once accepted, details are automatically inserted into the Outlook calendar."

"But that is just the start. We also attach a map of the location of the office to the email. The map also shows them the location of the parking space that will be specifically reserved for them when they visit. And every day my P.A. puts out 'Reserved For Mr. X' signs so that visitors are indeed greeted by an empty parking space with their name on it."

The result is that clients and prospects really feel valued and welcome. And that effect continues as they enter the building, where they are greeted in a comfortable reception area complete with a coffee table containing a stylish album of handwritten client testimonials. Since there is no other reading material in the reception area, visitors invariably read the album full of glowing tributes about the practice. "As a result of these little touches, people get a really positive impression of the firm even before the meeting starts," remarks Joe.

"They often comment on how impressed they are with the effort that has gone into making this basic experience stress free, distinctive and personal. And as a result they really feel appreciated, and they see us as special, so our meetings are more positive and it is much easier to justify higher fees than would otherwise be possible."

"I also know that many visitors take this positive experience away with them and recommend us to others because of it. And those referrals, of course, have been one of the key drivers of our growth."

Helping clients with their marketing

Unlike most accountants, Sole Associates offers a free marketing service to its clients. By joining the Academy for Growth and paying a monthly fee, the practice has exclusive use of the Academy's services in the Surrey area so that none of its competitors can do the same. As a result, it is able to give its clients various (locally) unique services to help them grow their business, including:

- a free marketing critique service
- a free marketing telephone hotline, and
- a free monthly marketing newsletter.

This, confirms Joe, has been a great success: "Offering marketing support has impressed clients enormously and sets us apart from other firms. Clients that have used the service have found it very effective. It has also helped us to convert prospective clients and justify higher fees. Existing clients often comment on how much they appreciate the effort we are making to help their business."

Getting paid properly by sole traders and partnerships

All sole trader and partnership clients are now advised annually on the tax savings they can make if they incorporate their business, and incorporation tax planning software is used to handle the calculations so the results can be seen immediately.

When this approach was first launched, Joe was unsure what price to quote for follow-up work. He explained: "I remember one client who made a profit of some £300,000, where the tax savings were projected to be around £20,000 per year, and I priced it at about 2.5 times our historical fees for this type of work. Since the client could see the actual tax savings presented live and in a professional way, they were very happy to pay the fee quoted."

Initial success with the service encouraged a bolder approach with value-based fees. For example, a value-based fee of £11,500 was quoted to one client although, since he was also a close friend, Joe offered to reduce this to £3,000. "His response, having seen the potential savings, was that he was actually happy to pay the full fee," Joe comments. "In fact, he insisted that we charged him the full amount. At the time that amazed me. But now I realise that clients are happy to pay high fees when the benefits are far higher still."

He added, "Because the software carries out the detailed calculations instantly in front of the client and presents the potential tax savings clearly, it makes it much easier for clients to appreciate the value of the advice being given. And that makes them much happier to pay proper fees so that we can do a proper job."

Charging what the job is worth

The practice's experience of pricing incorporations made it aware of the wider opportunities to quote fees based on the value of the work to them. Joe explains: "We have found that clients are generally happy to pay on this basis for all manner of work when they can see clearly that the benefits are very much larger than the fee. So wherever possible, that is how we price."

An example occurred when a team member identified the possibility of claiming Overlap Relief against prior year profits for two professional clients. This had been missed by their previous accountant and HMRC verbally confirmed that £25,000 was due to each client.

The team member suggested that a fee of £500 per client was appropriate for this work, but Joe disagreed: "Given the size of potential refund and the uncertainty that any claim would be successful, I suggested that we write to each client, explain the situation and quote them a fee of 25% of any tax refund. The team member was very sceptical of this approach and whether the clients would be willing to pay on those terms. However, the email was sent and both clients agreed to the fee basis. In fact, one of them actually said in their response that they hoped we earned a very large fee from this! The tax refunds have now been agreed with HMRC and our total fee for both clients amounts to approximately £12,500, which is a lot fairer to us than if we had gone with the first suggestion of only charging £500."

Improving billing and debtor collection

In addition to value pricing, Sole Associates has also made other changes to the way it calculates prices and is paid, including:

- Pricing software is now used to produce fixed price agreements in front of all new clients for situations where value based pricing is not possible.

- All new clients are now only given two options for payments: Direct Debit over ten months or Direct Debit collected on the 15th of each month for payment in full of any outstanding invoices. All existing clients, who were not paying by standing order, were contacted and asked to choose one of these two options. This gave the practice the opportunity to review and agree fixed fees for the year ahead using its pricing software.

- All clients currently paying by standing order are currently in the process of agreeing revised fees going forward and switching to Direct Debit collection.

The benefits of the new billing and collection approach

The changes to the billing and payment systems have had a profound effect on the practice:

- Clients appreciate the transparency and fairness of the pricing software.

- The pricing system has generated more work, since some clients have asked the practice to complete their bookkeeping so they can benefit from lower year-end accounting bills.

- The software enables the clear definition of the services to be carried out and, more importantly, ensures the practice is being paid an appropriate fee for it.

- To date, no client has questioned the price that appears on the screen. None have asked for a reduction although some try to reduce the fee in other ways, such as by agreeing to provide better quality records.

- In many cases, new and existing clients agree to higher fees for the same work because they can better appreciate what is involved. They often comment on how much more professionally, pricing of services is handled, compared to other firms.

- All Direct Debit agreements set the last instalment to be received around the time that end of year accounts are completed. This means that all fees are received in advance.

- The billing system has been simplified so that automated bills are raised to match Direct Debit instalments with a corresponding improvement in cash flow.

According to Joe: "Taken together these changes have literally transformed our cashflow and profitability."

An exit strategy that really works

Every business owner needs an exit strategy to ensure that, when the time for retirement arrives, their departure can go through smoothly and they can be properly rewarded for their contribution and effort over the years.

In the case of Stafford & Co, founder Ken Stafford's exit strategy was put to the test in November 2010, when he sold his shares in the practice and reduced his involvement to two days a week. And happily, it passed with flying colours.

According to Robert Stafford, who now drives the business: "Despite dramatically reducing the amount of partner level time available to get things done, the business has coped really well and service levels have not suffered at all. Without our focus over the last few years on involving our entire team in systemising and improving the business, I am sure this would not have been possible, as Ken's departure would have left a huge hole in our ability and capacity to deliver."

Three things in the diaries of every single team member

Bolton-based Stafford & Co has two Directors and six other members. Central to its ability to cope seamlessly with Ken's reduced involvement, are three key items that appear in everybody's diaries.

1. **Monday morning meetings** – Every week starts with a Monday morning team meeting, as Robert explains: "We plan the work for the week ahead, allocate responsibilities and ensure workloads are doable. We also make everyone aware of who we will be talking to and where we will be in the week so that we can spot opportunities for one team member to help another. For example, by knowing that a particular client is coming in, our credit control team can politely remind them about any outstanding payments and another team member can chase them for any outstanding information they need to serve that client better."

2. **Friday afternoon focus** – Having started the week with a planning session, "Every Friday, we all finish chargeable work at 1.30pm and spend the rest of the afternoon working as a team to implement systems, enhance efficiency and generally improve our practice."

3. **Monthly meetings** – The final element, which ensures team buy-in, is a monthly meeting. Key performance measurements, including all the practice's financial information, are recorded in a One Page Plan and are shared with the team at these meetings. "I can tell you, I was slightly

reluctant to share everything with them at first," remarks Robert. "But now we know it is the right thing to do, since the results speak for themselves."

Benefits enjoyed by all

The main benefit, for founder Ken Stafford, is that he has been able to greatly reduce his working week, knowing that the business will not suffer in any way as a consequence.

Other benefits have included:

- The ability to implement IRIS practice management software far quicker than expected, which has greatly improved management of workload, turnaround and planning of jobs

- Jobs being done more efficiently and quickly so that costs are reduced, service levels are improved and there is more time to add real value for clients

- Increased team member awareness of what the business is doing, the results that are being achieved, what is needed in order to become better and how they can contribute to those improvements

- Improved team spirit, motivation and morale since members feel more valued, trusted and involved.

Two director start-up that has grown to over £800,000 in 5 years

Since starting in May 2006, Stark Main, a two director practice that now employs 15 full time and 4 part time people in the Scottish Borders, has achieved the following:

- *Grown its fees to £776,000 in the year to May 2010 – £178k more than the previous year*

- *On target for £850,000 in the year to May 2011*

- *Generated average fees per client of £5,600*

- *Consistently wins an average of 3-4 ideal clients a month*

- *Has eliminated cashflow problems by collecting 60% of its total fees in advance by direct debit, and*

- *The directors get to take 11 weeks holiday a year*

In the notes that follow, Director Ian Main describes in detail exactly how they did it.

Right from the start we set out to differentiate ourselves by: becoming our clients' most 'trusted professional adviser'; focusing on added value services; being passionate about service excellence; building a team of people with a 'can do' attitude & commitment; working as a team; and running the firm as a 'business' in a commercially focused manner.

Entry level service package

We have a number of clearly defined service level offerings. For example, our entry level package specifies that in addition to the 'necessary evil' of annual compliance, every single one of our clients will receive all of the following as the bare minimum every year (and all of our clients do indeed receive at least this):

- Production of annual accounts and tax returns as required

- A diagnostic review of their key improvement opportunities (typically using our OnTrack software)

- A copy of the Performance Measurement and Improvement system, and at least an annual meeting to present and discuss the Financial Performance Review (i.e. 5 year trend analysis) report and Benchmarking report from the system, and to help them to develop an improvement action plan

- Pre year-end tax planning meeting

- An 'Entry level' BoardView service, whereby up to 4 hours of our time is available to them in a structured manner as and when they need it (NB: Our 'Strategic' BoardView service is the next stage up for clients looking for much more ongoing help from us. This is priced on a case by case basis, with our largest fee to date being £60,000 a year)

- Proactive and targeted mailers containing ideas, tips, insights, research findings and reports of relevance to them

- Free ad hoc helpline access to any member of our team

- A caring and professional service from our passionate team at all times

This combination of services and advice on improvement potential is the fundamental cornerstone of what makes us successful. We feel strongly that this is the approach required from the modern professional, and are proud to be actually delivering it, rather than merely paying 'lip service' to it within our marketing materials, as some firms seem to do.

Of course, we explain all of this very clearly to prospects, and as a result have found that:

- It differentiates us very clearly from other firms

- Clients who are looking for 'more' are naturally drawn to us

- Value is generally easily demonstrable and price sensitivity becomes much less of an issue.

- Our conversion rate for prospects exceeds 90% (see later for what else we do to achieve this)

- As a result we continue to engage an average of 3-4 ideal new clients per month, and our average fee per client has risen to £5,600

Inevitably, not every business in our area will want to work with us on these terms. However, that really doesn't matter to us at all, since we are happy for them to work with other more traditional accountants. The only question that matters to us is whether enough of the right kind of businesses want to work with us on those terms, and I can tell you the answer to that question is a categoric yes. Best of all, the kind of clients our approach appeals to, are the dynamic, entrepreneurial, forward thinking businesses that have a real future.

Of course we don't appeal to people who are treading water between jobs, price shoppers, timewasters and carrier bag jobs, but who cares? Those are not the kind of clients we want anyway, and I can tell you that life is so much more enjoyable without them.

Client care systems

In order to deliver the highest possible level of service, we have created formal client service teams, and all clients have an allocated Director, Manager and Technician. As a result:

- Each client has direct access to at least three named contacts via their direct telephone, email and mobile phone numbers, and service response times are always rapid as a result

- Each manager now has a defined portfolio of clients for which they have full responsibility

- Managers really get to know their clients as people and as businesses, understand their issues and needs, and are seen by clients as their main and most important contacts within the firm

- Our clients know with certainty that they will always receive continuity of service.

- Regular proactive contact is ensured through CRM reminders, with the most effective methods of communication (i.e. phone, fax, email, letter, face to face, newsletter etc) for each individual's preferences being identified

- Monthly proactive telephone calls/meetings are systematically scheduled with our A and B grade clients.

- Thank you notes and other messages of appreciation are sent whenever warranted

- The directors have been released from day to day operational matters, which has allowed them to focus on providing strategic/value added input

- And to make sure the whole thing is working, we measure, report and monitor the client's service metrics within each manager's portfolio, in terms of turnaround times, client satisfaction levels and financial performance

Happy and skilled team

In 2008 our entire team worked together to develop our mission statement, which is:

"We aim to be the leading firm of chartered tax advisors and accountants in the Scottish Borders and beyond with a happy and skilled team"

Everything we do is aligned clearly to this mission, and the "happy" and "skilled" team elements are focused upon on an ongoing basis. For example;

- We have banned the word "staff", with its connotations of "them and us", and instead refer to ourselves as the team, since we are all in it together.

- We operate an open culture; we meet as a full team every month for a development meeting, each team member takes a turn at chairing and directing these meetings and all have a chance to contribute to strategy at these meetings.

- We share openly our key performance indicators (KPI's) and finances on a One Page Plan at these meetings in a spirit of openness.

- We have created career development paths and have no 'glass ceilings', having created 19 jobs in 4 years since commencement, including 5 management positions.

- Our structure, with the partners not involved in much of the day to day technical work, automatically gives team members more exposure to interesting work and responsibility than is the case at many other firms.

- We take our team's health seriously and achieved Bronze award status under the Healthy Working Lives programme in 2010. As part of this we operate a bike to work scheme.

- We also take team happiness seriously. We use an electronic monitoring system (Team Matters) whereby all team members are required to complete a short questionnaire on a weekly basis and a more detailed one monthly. These reports are then automated and collated to allow a monthly analysis of each team member's happiness, and to identify any issues arising and provide support where required. We have targeted a minimum level of happiness of 4 out of 6 (i.e. a rating of 'excellent' happiness) and currently have a whole team average of 4.6 out of 6. When any individual's score is responded at a level of 3 or less the directors receive an instant email and text message to make them aware, and are afforded the opportunity to meet and discuss the potential issue with the individual team member. If no issues arise of this nature, the monthly reports are analysed and shared with the whole team at the development meeting.

Growing our people

Some of the things we do in order to ensure that our team members develop and grow as people and professionals include:

- We hold twice yearly individual appraisals and agree personal improvement plans.

- We hold 'on the job' project delivery appraisals and feedback after each engagement.

- We use in house 'role playing' sessions to build confidence and skills.

- We also create mentoring and shadowing opportunities daily, to allow team members to experience aspects of what the firm does that are new to them and build competence in those areas.

- We work hard to systemise the business using our System Builder software, and in the last 12 months a further 82 systems have been written and 62 systems implemented by the team. As well as leading to significant efficiency savings, these systems also allow team members to learn new skills and consistently deliver the very best service to clients.

- We have recently invested £6,000 in a management training needs analysis project in conjunction with a leading training provider. All directors and managers have been allowed to assess their skills and approach by way of psychometric and 360 degree appraisals and personal development plans have been agreed, based on the results.

- We invest heavily in internal training and external courses. All team members are offered 100% funding of training requirements and given additional holidays for exam and study purposes.

- 84% of our team are following professional studies at present.

- We have commenced an 'MBA Lite' training programme for the directors and managers in order to strengthen our strategic direction.

- We have set a monthly target of training hours and report both that, and our actual performance on our monthly One Page Plan.

- We agree as a whole team what training will be held in the next month and structure delivery of this, and agree actions and methods appropriately.

- Our electronic happiness monitoring system also provides a mechanism for team members to communicate their ideas for improving the business.

Supporting and rewarding our people

Some of the ways we support and reward our team include:

- Market leading remuneration levels
- Flexi time for all team members
- A flexible benefits package
- Holiday time bank
- Regular medical health checks and private healthcare scheme
- Remote working is an option for those who want it
- PDA/i-phone access to diary, email and remote access to server

- 100% of our management team are young mothers, and are afforded part time and additional flexible working practices to allow career progression alongside parental responsibilities
- An 'open door' policy for team access to the directorship team

The benefits from our team approach

As a consequence of our commitment to building a great team, and working together as a team, we have experienced the following benefits:

- Earned an excellent reputation as a firm
- Had a lot of fun, and a created a wonderful team spirit with genuinely happy team members who 'love' their job
- Were named as the Employer of the Year in the 2011 Scottish Borders Business Excellence Awards
- We have a 'waiting list' of suitable candidates looking to join our team as opportunity arises

In addition, the spectacular growth of the business is a direct consequence of the way we treat our people. We have provided a modern, dynamic and caring environment for our team. And they, in turn, have delivered a modern, dynamic and caring service to our clients.

Giving back to the community

We believe that being a modern professional involves social responsibilities as well as commercial opportunities. Some of the things we have done in order to try to meet these responsibilities have included:

- Investing over £20,000 in time a year in supporting the Princes Scottish Youth Business Trust, including acting as advisers and mentors to young entrepreneurs, fund raising, judging their 'Business of the Year' competition and sponsoring their 'Elevator Programme' that allows young businesses the opportunity to network. This is a big commitment, but we see it as an investment in the businesses of the future. Our involvement in these ways has also led to us meeting new clients with recurring fees of almost £52,000.
- We raised £5,518 for MacMillan Cancer Support when the whole team set out to scale the heights of Ben Nevis.
- We provide our services to a number of civic organisations on a charitable basis
- Our team members serve in treasurer or committee roles in a number of community clubs and organisations and provide professional support services to assist where possible.

Generating more leads, referrals and enquiries

We have done many things to successfully generate enquiries, leads and referrals, including:

- Running regular seminars on topics such as how to improve your profits and cashflow

- Running a one-off " Women in Business" Seminar, to celebrate Women's Enterprise Day. Eighty female entrepreneurs attended, it generated an incredible amount of goodwill and to date we have won four new clients as a result

- Acting as guest speakers at dozens of seminars and events run by other organisations

- Forging a strategic referral alliance with a leading Edinburgh law firm, who now subcontract £18,000 of recurring trust and personal tax compliance work to us, and have referred £45,000 of other tax planning work

- Creating a referral alliance with a high end contractor's logistics company, who refer 'C-Suite' executives to us for accounting and tax services

- Systemising our referral links with banks, invoice discounters and other financial organisations has led to over £100,000 of referral business

- We recruited a high quality Business Development Manager, and linked the cost directly to their success. This is working well for everyone, since in the first nine months they generated £45,000 worth of new clients for us

- The conversations we automatically have every year around our Performance Measurement and Improvement system, are a natural lead generator for additional services amongst our existing clients, as are the pre year-end tax planning meetings we have with every single client

- During the recession we have systematically offered to do cashflow projections for all of our clients, and almost 30% have taken up the offer and paid us good fees in the process

- Our management information systems show us exactly where our leads come from – and by identifying our 'rich seams' of new business we have been able to focus our marketing to 'mine' these fully.

Converting more leads into clients

Our strategy has always been 'not to be the cheapest, but to be the best'. We have therefore remained steadfastly proud of our track record of delivering value and resisted any urge to compete on price. In fact, we have increased our charges during the last year by an average of 10% across all service areas.

Of course, given that we charge premium prices, we have to provide prospects with compelling evidence that when they work with us they will receive a premium service. Some of the ways we do that include:

- Systematically searching for 'quick wins', such as tax planning opportunities that may have previously been missed, where the benefits are larger than our annual fee, thereby allowing us to make the point that working with us will in effect be free in the first year

- To help us identify these quick wins, we have invested in tax planning and profit improvement software that has been specifically designed to be used live in front of businesses. Very often the scope for improving things for them is enormous, since so few accountants give their clients enough of this kind of input

- And to maximise the impact of this software, we have invested in high quality LCD TV display equipment in our meeting rooms – which really creates a 'wow' effect, and greatly aids our lead conversion success

- As an example, we met a long established unincorporated business at the end of last year, and they said they were happy with their existing adviser of 15 years standing. But by using our Incorporation Tax Planner software at the meeting, we successfully converted them (at twice the annual cost they were currently paying) by showing them how we could save them over £19,000 a year in tax. Their existing accountant had mentioned incorporation and given them a 'leaflet', but had not made clear 'what was in it for them', so they had not gone ahead. Therefore the numbers we showed them were a revelation, and in addition to the annual fee for recurring work, they also asked us to do the core incorporation work at a fixed fee of £7,700, and do the work involved in capitalising goodwill for a value based fee of £22,000 (the tax savings were very large!). To date our average fee for incorporations runs at around £9,000, which would have been incredibly difficult to achieve without this methodology.

- We also guarantee our 'health check' type services, such that if the savings we identify are not greater than the fee, then the service will be free. In fact, on some occasions we have even guaranteed that the savings will be at least £100,000 (and even then we have never had a claim on the guarantee, which is a sad indictment of things that their previous advisers had missed).

The Stark Main sales system

In order to improve our sales lead conversion rate even further, we designed a five step system for selling "The Stark Main Way", and called it the GAMES process on account of the first letter of each step. The five steps are:

Greet – When a potential client arrives it is important to create an immediate rapport and positive experience to help relax and make them feel comfortable. So the system contains best practice for body language, attitude and what to say.

Ask – We then ask the potential client a series of carefully designed questions to help us find out exactly what their challenges are and identify their needs. We also establish why those things are important, and how important they are, quantifying it where possible. In this step the client is doing most of the talking, prompted and guided by our questions.

Match – Once we know what they really need, we show them the things that we can do that best match those needs. We do most of the talking, focus on advantages and benefits rather than features, and make recommendations.

Extras – In this step we aim to exceed their expectations, by giving them extra information, value, insights and recommendations. This in turn may result in them wanting to buy extra services from us.

Sell – And finally we need to close the sale. So the system sets out best practice for spotting the buying signals, asking for the business, and handling objections.

We created this system because we recognised that selling is both difficult and fundamental to the success of any business. We also recognised that successful sales people do things on purpose, and that their success is rarely accidental.

As a result of the GAMES process, our success is not accidental either.

Reclaiming NI paid by sleeping partners

Huddersfield sole practitioner Stead Robinson generated £4,000 in contingent fees with a relatively small amount of time costs, by helping three small clients submit claims to recover £21,700 of NI paid by their sleeping partners.

Within four weeks the first claim had been accepted without question by HMRC, the client's self assessment account had been credited with £10,064, and £1,500 of the contingent fee had become payable.

Here is the step by step process Stead Robinson used to generate these results:

STEP 1   They attended a Tax Club seminar and saw how easy it was to systemise the process of reclaiming NIC contribution paid by sleeping partners.

STEP 2   Immediately after the seminar a manager then went through their entire client database to identify partnerships where they thought there might be a sleeping partner (very often the sleeping partner was a spouse, of course). They also identified companies that had incorporated since 2005 and where prior to incorporation there might have been a sleeping partner (since NI paid by sleeping partners after 2004/5 could be reclaimed). The end result was a list of 20 clients where the manager thought there might be a sleeping partner and therefore that a reclaim might be possible.

STEP 3   The principal of Stead Robinson then reviewed the list and crossed off 17 clients where he knew that the "sleeping partner" did not actually qualify for a refund because they did too much in the business to be genuinely "sleeping." This left 3 clients where there was a genuine sleeping partner.

STEP 4   The principal then rang those three clients, explaining that it might be possible to get them a combined total of £21,700 of NI back. He also explained that it would involve putting in a claim going back as early as 2004/5. And finally, he explained that to make it a risk free process for them, he would only charge £250 per tax year that he was successful in getting them an NI refund. Across the three clients these contingent fees would total £4,000 if the full £21,700 was refunded by HMRC. All three of the clients said "yes" without hesitation – since for them there was nothing to lose and everything to gain.

STEP 5   Because they used The Tax Club system, doing all the calculations and submitting all the documentation was very straight forward. The total investment in time generated a four-fold increase on normal charge-out rates.

STEP 6   Within four weeks the first claim had been accepted without question by HMRC, the client's self assessment account had been credited with £10,064, and £1,500 of the contingent fee had become payable. And as I write up this case study a few weeks later, the other two refunds are expected shortly.

According to principal Philip Lofthouse: "Using a system made it all so easy. It takes away all the hard work, and allows us to concentrate on being really proactive with clients. That means that our clients are really happy with the refunds generated, at no risk and therefore happy to pay us the negotiated contingent fee."

He added: "The Tax Club is working brilliantly for us and for our clients. The seminars are excellent, sharing ideas with other members is invaluable, and the systems are an incredibly useful way of earning better fees by providing better tax solutions and service."

The seven keys to being an extraordinary start up

The Wow Company was started from scratch in 2004 by Peter Czapp, Simon Weeks and Paul Bulpitt. Today they have a vibrant practice that employs 12 people and, according to Peter, is taking the UK's small business community by storm.

According to Peter: "We have a fantastic client list of really cool small businesses, and earn highly profitable premium prices, that clients gladly pay because what they get in return is so much more valuable than from other accountants."

So what is the key to their success?

Peter's initial response was: "There is no single glib answer. It is a myriad of things really." But as we talked further it became clear that at least seven factors were vitally important to their success.

1. **Have a crystal clear picture of the ideal clients you want**

    They are crystal clear on the sectors and the size of businesses they want to work with. Peter explains why, "We recognise that we can't be brilliant at everything, so we've decided to focus on companies with turnovers under £2m. Because that's all we do, we've got really good at looking after them and really understand what they need. We've also built up expertise in a number of vertical markets. For example, we do a lot of work for creative companies in London. We know what makes them tick and can tailor our service to their needs."

    As a result of this clarity they are very selective about the clients they take on, and regularly turn down businesses that would like to appoint them but don't fit the ideal client profile.

2. **Design your service to meet the precise needs of your ideal clients**

    Having identified who they really want to work with, the next essential step was to work out exactly what those ideal clients really want and need from their accountant, and build their entire practice around delivering precisely that.

    For them, for example, that means insisting that every single new client meets them at least twice a year. "Two meetings a year is the bare minimum for pre and post year end planning. But quarterly meetings are more typical."

"Regular meetings are essential to really understanding clients, building relationships and delivering value. And we find people who are serious about their businesses are really happy to pay for the additional value this gives them."

Importantly, there are no compromises, as Peter explains: "If someone doesn't want that kind of regular input from us we will politely introduce them to a number-cruncher style accountant."

3. **Give them a ten-fold return on their investment**

"We aim to give all of our clients a 5-10 fold return on the fees they pay us. And really that isn't that hard to deliver. But rather than fall into the trap of over promising, we don't go public with that aim in order to win new clients. Instead we prefer to over-deliver once we win them as clients.

But even so, setting an internal target of giving clients a 5-10 times return on their investment in our fees, really focuses our minds on delivering amazing service (and tangible tax savings!)."

4. **Involve your team every step of the way**

None of this would be possible without the full support and involvement of every single person in the team. In the early days this was achieved by weekly team meetings to reinforce the vision, update everyone on the results and involve them in improving every aspect of the practice.

Now things are running smoothly, the team meetings only need to be held once a month. Regardless of frequency, openness and candour are the essential order of the day at these meetings. Day-to-day information is shared via an internal social media tool, called Yammer. This ensures everyone is immersed in the Wow culture every single day.

5. **Eliminate cashflow problems**

All of their clients pay by monthly direct debit. As well as almost completely eliminating debtor collection issues, this also has a powerfully positive effect on client service levels.

According to Peter: "Because they are paying us every month, we know that our clients are constantly judging us on what we have done for them that month. And that in turn focuses our minds on delivering an amazing service, month in month out – with regular contact, genuine proactivity, and the constant drip drip of real value."

6. **Aim to knock their socks off**

"The key is to deliver amazing service that knocks their socks off. That way clients are happy to pay the fees, be 100% loyal and tell everyone they know about you," says Peter.

"Of course we don't always succeed, but rather than see them as failures, the key is to see disappointments as learning opportunities that help us improve our systems and procedures so that we continually get better and better."

7. Really set ourselves apart from the competition

Peter is adamant that it is essential to differentiate yourself from the competition in order to achieve real success. He is also clear that these differentiators need to be embedded in the habits, culture, systems and processes of a firm – as opposed to being merely "flavour of the month" gimmicks. Understandably, though, he asked me not to divulge any of his key differentiators in this article, since they represent the essence of his competitive advantage.

The really interesting question, however, is not what Peter's long list of differentiators is – but whether most firms have any such differentiators at all? In my experience they do not!

And yet as the ICAEW's excellent "The profitable and sustainable practice" report says: "To make more profit than the rest you must be different, and your clients and prospective clients must know that you are different."

Better clients, better meetings and better tax planning

Since 2009 Thoburn and Chapman, a long established 13 person practice in South Shields run by Ralph Thoburn Junior, has:

- Quadrupled profits

- At the same time they have reduced client numbers from over 100 to just 75

- Eliminated an overdraft they had needed for "as long as anyone can remember"

- Won prestigious business awards

- "The practice was started by my father many years ago, and I know he would be tremendously proud of what we are now achieving," said Ralph.

According to Ralph there are seven keys to this turnaround in fortunes.

Learn from others

"None of us will ever come up with all the best ideas ourselves, and we shouldn't even try," explains Ralph. "Which is why we regularly get together to swap ideas and insights with other really successful accountants, and why we also have a coach who both shares his insights and ideas with us, as well as helping us to work out things for ourselves and actually turn it all into action. Together they have made a huge difference, and I think every practice should do this."

Grading clients

At one of those idea swapping sessions, Rob Walsh of Clear Vision (see Example of Excellence 8) encouraged Ralph to grade his clients, and structure his service offerings around the needs of each grade. So, using a standard system, Ralph settled on:

- **Gold clients** – who need 3 or 4 structured meetings a year, the cost of which is factored into their fixed fee

- **Silver clients** – who need a minimum of 2 meetings a year, again costed into the fixed fee

- **Bronze clients** –who only need an annual meeting

- **Tin and Bin clients** – who they either educated into becoming gold/ silver/bronze, or exited from the practice altogether

"This process has increased our total fees and our average fees per client, improved the quality of our client base, and made our working lives more enjoyable and satisfying."

Fixed price agreements

"All our clients are now on Fixed Price Agreements, with a system of Extra Work Orders for things not covered by the agreements," explains Ralph.

And since this new pricing approach often meant clients paying more, Ralph was very careful in the way he introduced it:

- "We started with the easy cases first – new clients and existing clients where we had a really strong personal relationship. And only moved on to the trickier cases when we were more confident"

- "It is much easier to get a 'yes' when you are face to face – so wherever possible we brought it up at meetings rather than in writing or on the phone"

- "We recognised that some clients would not want to switch to the new approach the first time we told them about it – so we were happy to bide our time, and gently remind them each time we met"

- "Using the Times Up! pricing software systemised the whole process, and we would have been lost without it."

They also get their clients to pay up front, usually via direct debit. And where that isn't possible, they tend to work with a specialist finance company so that the practice gets paid in full up front, while the client is able to pay by instalments.

Standard meeting agendas

In order to ensure consistently high levels of service, and that nothing important is ever missed or glossed over, they use standard agendas for all meetings. These agendas cover four main areas:

1. Accounting and audit issues

2. Advanced tax planning – to improve the client's tax bills

3. Wealth creation – to add to the client's wealth by, for example, making their businesses more successful and profitable

4. Wealth management – to make the most of their wealth once they have created it

Their agendas always also include three key questions:

1. **What else do you want us to talk about today?** – This is asked at the start of the meeting, not at the end, since if the client has a burning issue it is vital that it is dealt with before anything else on the agenda

2. **How are we doing?** – Proactively checking that the customer is happy with the service they are receiving, means that any problems can be corrected quickly, and prevented from festering into something far worse

3. **Do you know anyone you can introduce to us?** – By asking for referrals whenever the customer has just said that they are happy, Ralph and his team end up receiving more referrals.

"Importantly we also make sure clients know there is no charge for phoning us between meetings," explains Ralph, "and we repeat the message whenever we see them. Since the more times they phone us with problems, the more times we can help them with solutions. Solutions that we use Extra Work Orders to charge extra fees for."

Wealthy Creations LLP

"Until relatively recently, genuinely leading edge advanced tax planning wasn't possible for firms like us, and clients like ours," says Ralph. "But through our membership of various accountancy associations we are now able to access some of the UK's best tax brains and strategies, and our clients are so grateful since the tax savings can be jaw-dropping at times. And we benefit very substantially too, since the tax experts we work with gladly share some of their fees with us, and these 'payaways' can be very sizeable."

To distinguish this new type of service from his core business, Ralph set up Wealthy Creations LLP. It has been such a success that its turnover is now equivalent to a third of the GRF of the practice.

Ralph generates interest in this type of tax planning by:

- Systematically data mining his client and prospect data base to identify who could potentially benefit from the advance tax strategies available

- Adding "Advise client of their next tax payable" to every meeting agenda – since this reminds them of the pain involved in paying tax

- Making the next item on the agenda "Tax minimisation strategies" – since this juxtaposition helps them to understand that there are "painkillers"

- "We are also fastidious about making sure that our clients fully understand the risks as well as the rewards from this type of tax planning."

"Once you understand and accept that this type of tax planning is not going to appeal to everyone, it becomes hugely satisfying" says Ralph. "Since for those clients that it does appeal to, the benefits can be so large as to be genuinely life changing."

For example, one of Ralph's new clients saved enough in tax to be able to use the extra cash generated to rescue an ailing business and save over a hundred local jobs. While for Ralph it meant more than £100,000 in fees.

Laminated tax savings sheets

One of the most effective ways Ralph gets clients interested in advanced tax planning is to always carry around an A4 laminated sheet containing a worked example showing the various ways to extract profits from a company. It also shows how much tax they will pay under each of the options, how much net cash the business owner will get in their own bank account and what the effective tax rate is in each case.

He uses the sheet with clients and prospects. For example, this is how he uses it with prospects:

STEP 1   He takes a written agenda to every meeting, since (a) it shows he is professional enough to prepare properly for the meeting, and (b) it gives his meetings a clear structure, and acts as an aide-mémoire to ensure that he does all the right things at each meeting. NB: Ralph actually uses the "Agenda for sales meeting with target" from his System Builder knowledge base.

STEP 2   The written agenda doesn't specifically mention tax, since that would be to presume that he knows in advance what they are interested in. Instead, one of the questions it prompts him to ask is "What frustrations do you have when working with accountants?" (and, as part of his system, Ralph also has a list of the nine most common frustrations). Usually the answer includes words to the effect "We pay too much tax." But if it doesn't, he will ask further questions such as "How happy are you with how much tax you pay?" And as soon as they indicate that they would like to pay less tax, he immediately takes out the laminated sheet...

STEP 3   ...and uses it to summarise their full range of profit extraction options. In particular he uses it to show how much smaller their tax bills will be with an Employee Benefit Trust, and how much more net cash they will have in their pockets as a result.

Important note: *This part of the case study was written up before the December 2010 changes relating to EBTs. However, the principles still apply to the currently available advanced profit extraction strategies.*

STEP 4   He also briefly outlines what will happen if they die tomorrow – making it clear that their IHT bills will also be much lower where they have used an EBT

STEP 5   If he has succeeded in grabbing their attention, and they want to find out more (which is almost invariably the case), he will then open up his Remuneration Tax Planning software on his laptop and use it to produce an instant personalised calculation of exactly how much tax they can save by changing the way they extract their profits.

Interestingly, he has found that he gets much better results if he uses the generic example on the laminated sheet to grab their attention, and then uses on screen tax calculator software to provide evidence of specifically how much they can save.

When explained in this step by step way, it is clearly a simple process that every accountant should and could be using with every single corporate client and prospect.

But Ralph has found: "Most prospects we meet have never had their full range of options spelled out with this kind of clarity. So when we use the laminated sheet to show them what is possible they are often stunned. They say things like 'why hasn't my accountant told me about this'. And they ask us to help them. So it is now something we do with every single prospect, since it greatly increases our chances of turning them into clients. And the really exciting thing is that it works best with really good clients – i.e. the ones with high profits. So it is not just helping us to win us new clients, it is actually helping us to win the right kind of new clients."

Enter business awards

To capitalise on and leverage their success, the firm appointed its founder, Ralph Thoburn Senior, as an "Awards Champion" whose job it was to enter them into business awards. As a result they were named North East Independent Firm of The Year, and were runners up in the national Accountancy Age Small Firm of The Year competition.

According to Ralph: "Winning those types of accolades really helps when pitching for new business. It also helps to remove resistance to our fees, even when we are more expensive. Since in both cases, people say things like, 'if your peers think you are special, you must be' shortly before they also say 'yes'."

He adds, "the other big benefit is that it makes us all even more proud to work here."

How to be proactive systematically

Wilds is an award winning 5 partner firm in Manchester that has put proactivity at the heart of what it does.

Making proactivity possible

Partner Mick Seddon explains: "We realised that one of the main obstacles to being truly proactive is partner workloads. In other words, partners are always so busy that there is rarely enough time to be as proactive as clients want us to be. So we knew we had to do something to change that."

The first thing they did was to brainstorm the main things that the partners currently did. Of the 21 most time consuming tasks that they identified, 17 were administrative or lower grade technical in nature (i.e. raising bills, writing letters, dealing with minor issues etc) and only 4 were seriously technical. "So I said to my colleagues," explained Mick, "it doesn't really make commercial sense to have the most expensive people doing the least valuable tasks, does it? And they agreed."

As a result, in 2008 they fundamentally changed the structure of the business, promoting seven of their team members to the new role of Customer Service Manager ('CSM'). These CSMs are now solely responsible for many of the 17 tasks the firm identified that the partners should not be doing (with most of the others being passed to the admin team), including:

- Planning the work, and managing the service

- Keeping the client informed

- Agreeing prices and raising bills

- Dealing with all compliance work

- Co-ordinating their clients' awareness of new services and other ways that the firm can help

New clients are introduced to their CSM right at the very start of the relationship. And they candidly explain that "Under the traditional way of running an accountancy firm, the more successful a partner is, the worse service inevitably becomes, because there is less of their time available to each client. So this is how we make sure that doesn't happen here."

According to Mick: "Clients are very happy with this approach because it means they get a better service. And our team loves it too, since those who have already been made CSMs see it as a great career move, and for the others it is an exciting career path to aspire to. In many traditionally structured firms some of the people we have made CSMs would never have been given this kind of responsibility. But that would have been such a waste, since they have all stepped up to the mark."

"Of course, you have to be realistic, and CSMs will occasionally make mistakes. We all do. So you need a two stage plan for that eventuality. Firstly, you minimise the occurrence by giving them proper training, systems and support. And secondly you minimise the consequences by having a supportive culture rather than a blame culture, recognising that most errors are systems failures, going the extra mile to put things right in this particular instance, learning from the episode, and improving the systems accordingly so that it doesn't happen again."

For the partners the big benefit from the CSM model is that it frees up a great deal of their time. "The exact amount of time saved varies from partner to partner," explains Mick, "but in my case, for example, it equates to one week a month."

Making proactivity happen

As a result of these changes, the partners now have more time to concentrate on other more important things, such as business development, strategy, and improving service by adding value and being proactive. Some of the ways they achieve the latter include:

- Providing free training on issues such as raising finance, improving cash flow and profits, and other major topical issues, along with paid-for management training either in a group or on a one to one basis. For example, over the last twelve months more than 50 businesses have been helped by their group mentoring sessions alone.

- Running quarterly "Crossroads" events that are typically attended by over 50 clients and potential clients. These events give attendees access to outside speakers, often on matters that they might not have considered, such as the use of a PR company, or how a PLC organises its reporting.

In addition, they have introduced a two stage proactivity system that is used by every CSM with every client:

- **Before the year end** – Three months before the client's year end the CSM meets the client and uses a TaxAbility checklist to identify opportunities to manage their tax affairs better and/or reduce their tax exposure.

- **After the year end** – Three months after the year end they meet again, and this time the CSM uses a "Cross helping toolkit" system. Essentially this system involves asking a series of about 15 questions that have been carefully designed to identify the issues, challenges and opportunities that the client wants to tackle. And once an issue is identified, the CSM simply asks "Would you like us to help you with that?" If the client says 'no', they still give the firm credit for offering to help. And if the client says 'yes', then the CSM has made a sale and now only has to agree the terms.

According to Mick: "It is still early days with this two stage proactivity system, but in the first six months, it not only impressed a lot of clients, but also directly led to £27,500 of extra work for us. So we expect it to become one of the key success factors in our business."

"To give you an example of its power, we have one client who had only ever bought a pure compliance service from us, and had previously resisted all our attempts to do more for him. But the three month meeting process went so well that they have now asked us to do various things for them, including IHT planning. And, I can tell you, that is a real breakthrough."

Pricing that supports proactivity

According to Mick: "The key is to operate in such a way that clients know that they can contact you and keep you informed at all times, and you can do the same to them, without them incurring a financial penalty (i.e. an extra fee arising from a ticking clock). This gives us the chance to provide good, timely and proactive advice, keep the client happy and away from problems, and also creates the opportunity for us to earn additional fees for additional work where this is warranted, without any risk of falling out with the client."

In practice, this means that Wilds have adopted a pricing methodology based on:

- Abandoning time sheets in favour of fixed fee arrangements
- Including within those fixed fees the facility for clients to make unlimited phone calls to their CSM and partner for quick advice
- Also including the pre and post year end meetings within the fee, and
- Charging prices that properly reflect the quality, scope and value of the service being provided

"This approach means that there are no barriers to a client contacting us with a problem, or us approaching them with an idea" says Mick. "And where this leads to an identifiable project (which it often does) then an extra work order can be generated and a fee agreed for the work, which we may not previously have even known about. Which is good for the client and good for us."

Start up sole practitioner with average fees of £8,900 per client

Alan Woods is a sole practitioner from the Wirral who started his practice, Woods Squared, from scratch in January 2007. Since then Woods Squared has attracted 30 clients with average fees of £8,900 per client. As a result it now employs 5 people, including Alan.

Woods Squared's other notable achievements include:

- Turnover grew by 21.3% in 2009 and 60.2% in 2010

- 100% of its clients are on a fixed fee and pay in advance

- Client satisfaction feedback scores are currently averaging 9.32 out of a maximum of 10

- In the last 12 months they have generated lifetime tax savings for clients totalling £2,576,276

- The nine key new things they have done in the last two years

When I asked Alan what have been the keys to his success during the last two years he reflected, discussed it with his team, and then came back and described in detail the following nine steps.

STEP 1   On 9 January of 2009 he presented his vision for the business to a "Mastery" group of partners from other accountancy firms that he meets with regularly to share ideas and insights. "This was a great exercise for us, since it really forced me to think about what I wanted to build and achieve, and what was most important to me. It gave me an enormous amount of clarity and focus. And the constructive criticism from my peers was also invaluable in weeding out sloppy thinking. So our vision became much sharper, incisive and inspiring as a consequence."

This process resulted in the team:

- Identifying their core values as "Quality, Innovative, Fun, Supportive and Proactive."

- Articulating their core purpose as "To work with owner managed businesses to help them grow and achieve their business and personal goals."

- Agreeing their 20 year goal as "To become the Aston Martin of our industry."

STEP 2 To help make the vision a reality, on 31 January he produced his first monthly One Page Plan. Some of the things he started measuring on it were:

- % of jobs completed within thirty days
- Client and team member happiness scores
- Number of improvement suggestions received from the team
- Number of referrals received
- Value of Extra Work Orders generated from existing customers
- Lowest fee (which at the time was £600, and they set themselves a target of £1500)
- Average fee per client
- Average grade of client

STEP 3 In March 2009, he carried out a client grading exercise, discovering that 27% were As, 41% were Bs, another 27% were Cs, and 5% were Ds. "As a result," explains Alan, "we set a target of having no D clients and many fewer C clients. And by September 2009 we had stopped acting for every single D client and two thirds of the C clients."

He adds, "We carried out another client grading exercise in January 2011, and now have 92% of our clients as As and Bs, with the other 8% being Cs."

STEP 4 Next, they clarified the structure of the business and the services that they wanted to offer to their clients. "Stemming from our vision we knew that we wanted to concentrate on added value services. And we also knew that we wanted a structure that was based on fewer clients per client manager – so we set an ideal limit of 25 clients per client manager paying us an average of £10,000 each."

STEP 5 To tie in with these plans they then introduced a minimum service level for all new clients – i.e. no one can now become a client unless they are willing to have (and pay for) BoardView meetings with Woods Squared at least once a quarter and a tax planning review on an annual basis.

STEP 6 Next they started to communicate the changes to the market by, among other things, getting a lot more press coverage.

STEP 7   In response to the recession really starting to bite, at the start of 2010 they launched a new 'Access to Finance' service to help clients obtain finance and funding. "We have had a huge amount of interest in it, and I am proud to say that we have a 100% success record in using it to help our clients actually obtain finance. This service is offered on a fixed fee basis and offers huge value as it includes all meetings/discussions with the various funding organisations, which allows us to tailor the information provided in each situation, rather than us just preparing another pretty (useless!) report."

STEP 8   "In early 2010 we also made the decision to further invest in the development of our team," says Alan. "So, as well as taking the entire team to Lapland to say thank you for what they had already helped us to achieve, we also psychometrically profiled our team using the DISC system. The insights this has provided to everyone in the team about how best to work together have been invaluable. So much so, in fact, that we now also use it as part of our recruitment system, and we even offer it as a service to clients."

STEP 9   In the summer of 2010 the firm moved to bigger and smarter premises in a listed building. As a result the team now has a much better working environment, a kitchen, a chill out room to watch TV or read, a games room for pool and darts, a gym area and shower facilities to even give them the option of cycling or running to work. "The move has had a really positive impact on morale."

There are also three meeting rooms, including one that can be used for seminars for up to 30 people. "We also invite clients and contacts to hold their meetings in our meeting rooms as another form of added value. And this has already helped one of them to secure a huge contract – which they might not have won if they had been forced to cram 7 people into their small office for the meeting!"

Alan summarised by saying: "These are the nine key new steps we have taken in the last two years. They were not necessarily big steps, but even baby steps can take you a long way if you take one after the other!"

Other keys to their success

In addition to the above nine steps, Alan confirmed that the firm has continued to do a number of other things that continue to make a major contribution to its success. They include:

- **Measuring team happiness** – "We use software called Team Matters to systematically measure real time and monthly team member happiness scores, and also to capture their ideas for improving the business. Not only does this show that we care and value their input, but it also allows us to deal with problems and capitalise on opportunities very quickly, which is great for morale and profitability."

"And for the record, our latest team happiness scores from Team Matters were 5.6 out of a maximum of 6."

- **Fixed Price Agreements** – "We use the Times Up pricing software to produce Fixed Price Agreements for all our clients, and I think now, more than ever, that this has helped us be different in the eyes of the new clients that we have been signing up. Crucially those fixed fees are paid in full before we start the work, so debtors and cashflow are never a problem."

- **Diagnostic reports** – "Every year every client receives a Key Improvement Possibilities report that we create using our OnTrack diagnostic review software. As part of this process we also benchmark them, and talk them through our findings and reports at their year end accounts meeting. We also ask them for nagging rights to make sure that they actually do the things on their action plans, and if they don't do them, we then offer our support to help them get things done. Not only is this genuine proactivity in action, which clients love, but it often also results in them wanting to buy additional support and services from us."

- **Incorporation tax planning software** – "Shockingly, we find that there are still many businesses that have not been properly or fully advised on the benefits of incorporation. So we have often been able to obtain new clients by using software live in front of them to demonstrate the savings they can make from incorporation."

- **Window of Opportunity charts ('WOO')** – "WOO charts are one of the most important, and at the same time simplest, tools that we use. Essentially they are just a spreadsheet that lists all of our clients down one axis, and all of our services and solutions on the other axis. We then colour in the boxes that represent the things each client is currently buying from us, and the blanks are our windows of opportunity. Of course, we regularly review our WOO chart, and have found it a great tool for helping to spot the extra areas where we can help our clients. And because we know that all of the services on the chart will all add huge value to our clients, it does not feel at all pushy when we mention these services to our clients, and they are always grateful that we are identifying other ways that we can help. As a result, it often leads clients to buy more from us."

"In fact, WOO charts are such a powerful concept that we also give talks at business seminars about how owner managed businesses can use them in their businesses too. And when we combine that with using our Business Potential sensitivity software to show them the positive impact on their profits of increasing their prices, most business owners get very excited. Yes, to us it may seem like simple stuff. But to them it is often a revelation."

- **Network membership** – "The tools, software, insights, systems and training we have received as a result of our membership of AVN have been central to our success. Put simply, we wouldn't have been able to achieve anywhere near as much without them. For example, they provided the Mastery group in Step 1, the One Page Plan system in Step 2, and the client grading system in Step 3. They also created the diagnostic review software, pricing software, tax planning software, sensitivity software and Team Matters software that we use to make our lives so much easier and our service so much better. But perhaps most importantly of all, they have provided the inspiration, motivation, encouragement and support we really needed to actually make things happen."

Example of how to generate an extra £20,000 in GRF from one client

Finally, by way of example, here is the story of how Alan turned one of his small clients into a £25,437 annualised recurring fee.

The client was a two person consultancy company, and their core service was based on the two shareholder-directors standing up and making presentations. At the outset they were turning over around £22,500 a month, and paying Alan £5,500 a year for a core compliance service consisting of bookkeeping, quarterly meetings, annual accounts and tax planning.

The problem was that the growth of the business was limited by the fact that there were only so many presentations that two people could deliver. So Alan showed one of the directors a video of Michael Gerber talking about how to work on your business, rather than in it, to create systems so that other people can do things to the same standard that currently only the business owners can. Whilst that director got very excited about the prospect, the other director (who lived 200 miles away and so didn't see the video) was understandably sceptical, since "surely no one else will be able to do it as well as us, or even properly." So nothing too much happened for six months. "With hindsight, I realise now that it is vital to get your message across to all the directors – so I should have shown the video to both directors at the outset," says Alan.

But things started to change in December 2008 when one of the Directors suddenly lost his voice. Then there was no choice, they had to adapt. And successfully coping with temporarily losing one of the two key presenters proved to them that it was possible to run the business in a way that wasn't dependent on the founders.

From that point onwards the Directors knew that they wanted to create a systems-based business, so that they could leverage their time and expertise, give themselves a better work-life balance and expand the business by bringing on board other presenters.

Initially they accepted Alan's offer of a Business Edge programme – i.e. a series of six £500 half day meetings to begin to identify, and create an action plan, for addressing the key issues within the business. Alan used the AVN Business Edge process and tools for this, but as they say, "other similar diagnostic processes are also available."

This process started in March 2009, and as it began to deliver value to the client – evidenced by the fact that their turnover increased from £22,500 to £50,000 a month between April and August – the client started to indicate that they wanted more help to ensure that they actually did the things on their action plan. It wasn't so much that they wanted Alan to do the things on their action plan for them. Instead they wanted him to make sure that *they* did the things on their action plan, since they knew that they were very busy and that it would be easy to let things slip. So more than anything else they wanted Alan to make them accountable.

Alan therefore suggested his Virtual Finance Director service to them, and presented them with a draft Fixed Price agreement to show them how much their investment would need to be. This is a flexible service that has a variety of possible elements from which the clients can pick and tailor to reflect their precise needs.

For your information, by the Autumn of 2009 17% of Alan's clients were already buying this Virtual FD service at an average package price of £25,000, and by early 2011 the take up rate had risen to 22%. And the typical mix of deliverables his clients select as they tailor the service to their own needs are:

- Monthly management accounts
- Monthly One Page Pan (or rolling cashflow forecasts if cash is the overriding issue)
- Monthly BoardView style board meeting attendance (larger clients also tend to want a monthly meeting with the management team to help them understand what is going on, and what they need to do next)
- And they also want him to play a "nagging" kind of role – i.e. to make them accountable so that they actually did the things that they had committed to doing

This is also exactly the mix of support that this particular client opted for under the "Virtual FD" banner. And, as a result, Alan has turned a £5,500 a year client into a £25,437 a year one.

Professionals are patient

"One big lesson I learned from this client," says Alan, "is to take it one step at a time, and not to be impatient. If the time is not right for the client now, it will be later. Keep reminding them gently of what else is possible in their business, and how you can help them with it. Keep proactively providing them with ideas, food for thought and evidence that there is a better way. But be happy to wait until they are ready. Sooner or later their circumstances and/or mindset will change, just as they did when one of the directors lost his voice, and at that point you will be the first person they turn to for help."

Is this the bravest (and most honest) thing an accountant has ever done?

Just over a year ago I received an email from Ian Bavill, who runs a small practice in Leeds, that quite simply left me speechless. The email itself is reproduced with his permission below. But to summarise, this is what had happened that day...

...The day before, Ian had been a delegate at my "Proactivity" seminar. First thing the next morning he emailed every single client apologising for not being proactive in the past, promising that things would now change, and by way of proof, offering to carry out a diagnostic review to identify new ways to put extra money in their bank account through better tax planning etc.

And by the time he emailed me at 4:22pm the same day:

- Almost all of his clients had replied positively, thanking him for his refreshing honesty, and accepting his offer

- Two clients had agreed in principle to double their annual fee

- Two prospects had agreed to meet him even though he said he would not be cheaper than their existing accountants, because he was now able to give them the kind of proactive input they really wanted

- And three clients had said they wanted more tax planning help

As a result, I consider Ian to be the bravest and most honest accountant I have ever met.

So when I talked to Ian again a few months later, I was really keen to see what had happened since. In addition to the above, Ian explained that as a result of sending out his email, and the new type of dialogue it created:

- Two clients had paid him £14,000 of extra fees for SIPP planning

- Another two clients had started paying him a total of almost £8,000 pa extra for management accounting services

- And they have not lost a single client

5 reasons why it is the right thing to do

I should stress that at no time had I ever suggested that Ian (or any other practitioner) write to their clients in this way. And I am sure that before I had heard Ian's story, I would not have been brave enough to do it personally. But now I think it is actually a really powerful idea. And I can think of at least five reasons why other firms should consider following Ian's lead.

Reason 1: Research – More than anything else, research shows that clients want their accountants to be proactive. But research also shows that most accountants merely pretend that they are proactive. They plaster the word across their promotional material. But are too busy to make genuine proactivity a central part of the habits, culture and systems of the firm. So at the moment, most accountants are not giving clients what they really want. But that is now changing rapidly, as more practitioners recognise the need to make genuine proactivity a priority.

Reason 2: Honesty – Those accountants who persist in falsely claiming to be proactive will increasingly be viewed by their clients as lacking two of the essential pre-requisites for being a trusted adviser: integrity and honesty. While those who come clean, tell the truth, and then change things for the better, will be trusted and respected.

Reason 3: Differentiation – Given that genuine proactivity is what clients really want, those accountants that rise to the challenge will make themselves so much more attractive to clients and prospects. And that in turn will make it much easier for them to win new clients and earn more from existing clients.

Reason 4: Momentum – Many practitioners already know what they need to do to make things better for them and their clients. For them the problem is not the knowing, but the doing. And the two main obstacles that prevent them doing what they know needs to be done are: they don't start, and/or they don't persevere. But Ian's approach overcomes both of these obstacles. It gives you a quick and simple way to start. And it ensures that, once you have started, you carry on, since it is very difficult to go back!

Reason 5: Profitability – Ian's actions have helped to substantially improve his profits. Remember, he did not lose a single client. Instead, many of them are now willingly paying higher prices and buying additional services.

Perhaps start small at first...

If sending an Ian Bavill style message to every client is too much for you, why not test the principle by starting small. For example, why not start with only a handful of clients. And instead of being honest with them in writing, convey the same message verbally. That way you are not holding yourself a hostage to fortune, you can fine tune your message, and you can react intelligently and in real time to whatever they say, so as to nip any problems in the bud and build on the really positive aspects.

To me that kind of test makes a great deal of sense.

But there is a VERY BIG WARNING... before you start having these kinds of conversations with clients you must make absolutely sure that you really can and will be more proactive in the future!

Email from Ian Bavill

Hi Steve

Thanks again for the seminar on Wednesday, it was a real eye opener. I returned home and didn't sleep until 2am as I had so much flying round in my head, and then arrived at work on Thursday morning with a real spring in my step and an enthusiasm for something I have not felt since the day I was stood in the departures lounge of Heathrow airport when I was about to embark on my year long travels of the world.

This may sound like a strange way to go, but this morning I emailed every single client of mine with an apology for not being proactive in the past and with a promise that things will change. By way of saying sorry I have arranged that each and every one of them will get an hour of my time for free, and a full diagnostic report of their business to discuss at the meeting. Pretty much all of them have replied, thanking me for being so honest, and taking me up on my offer. Once I have the software in place I will be getting on with this and see where it takes us. Two clients have called me and have agreed that if I follow through with my promise of a new improved service they would be willing to double their annual fee payable to me!!!

In addition I received two calls from prospects that a current client has sent my way, both looking for a cheap accountant. I told them they were looking in the wrong place and why, and they still want to meet as their current accountant is neither cheap nor good.

On top of this I have three clients interested in tax planning work. This is all before I've even implemented anything at all!!! Many thanks

Kind regards

Ian Bavill

The other key factor in their success

At the time of writing, 39 of the firms in this book work with AVN, and attribute much of their success to that fact.

Initially, therefore, some of the firms were kind enough to make explicit reference to this fact in their explanations of their success. However, on reflection, I was concerned that some readers may see this as partisan, and use it as an excuse for not taking the Examples of Excellence seriously. That was a risk I was simply not willing to take. So just prior to publication I took the decision to remove all these references, and put them in this appendix instead.

Of course, having already agreed the wording of these references with the firms in question, I was not able to change them in any way. Therefore I have simply removed the relevant passages from the Examples of Excellence and reproduced them in full here instead for completeness.

Example of Excellence 2
Keith Anderson of Anderson Advantage

Doubling turnover and taking Fridays off

A major driver for all this change was Keith joining AVN. But he admits that he could not initially make the AVN principles work, and now puts this down to him not really making any changes.

However, as he explains, "Once I became really committed to change I started reaping the benefits, and am now enjoying both my business and my life much more as a result. Having turned 60, I only wish I had started changing sooner!"

Example of Excellence 5
Marc Lawson of businessVision

How a small accountancy practice prospered in adverse conditions

"The other key for us has been AVN's System Builder software, which is used by every single team member and is constantly open on their desktops. We've added hundreds (if not thousands) of our own systems and resources to it as we've gone along but still have some way to go. And as a result, at the push of a button it shows us exactly what to do in almost every conceivable situation.

So we never have to reinvent the wheel, or make things up as we go along, since we always have proven best practice systems to follow. Which means we can give our clients better and quicker service, thereby driving up client loyalty at the same time as driving down our costs."

Example of Excellence 6
Nick Hume of Calcutt Matthews

How an established firm with a previously stagnant fee base achieved 28% and 21% fee growth in the last two years

"None of what we have achieved would have been possible three years ago. And it has only become possible since then because of AVN," explains Nick.

"They have supplied us with the inspiration training to set our goals and launch our Train To Gain funded One Page Plan and Business Improvement Planning services. They showed us how to set up our bonus scheme. They found us our business coach. They lined us up with all the tax specialists we now work with. And they have been instrumental in just about all the other things we have done that have improved our results over the last two years."

"If any practitioner thinks this all sounds too good to be true, I invite them to contact me. I will answer candidly any questions you have so that (a) you can see that it is all true, and (b) so that you can work out how to get the same or better results yourself."

In the first instance he has suggested you email him on nick.hume@calcutt-m.co.uk.

Example of Excellence 7
Kim Farrell of CBHC

16 partner firm focuses on innovation

"Our membership of AVN really augmented and assisted us in developing our Business Advisory Services, and the research and evidence they presented to us about the industry, gave us the impetus to continue down this new avenue.

The suite of tools it provided us really made us standout from our local competitors and are now at the core of our business like traditional accounting, audit and tax compliance."

Example of Excellence 9
Paul Miller of Cornish Accounting

Sole practitioner who no longer feels the need to do everything personally

"Many of the changes have been inspired by what we have learned from AVN and enabled by the tools and support it provides. It feels like the last 12 months have been a giant leap," says Paul, adding: "We now face the future with confidence and optimism. Team members and principal now have more fun. The process has been emotionally and physically uplifting and we all look forward to continuing that journey."

Example of Excellence 18
Glyn Davison of Harlands

A three pronged approach to serving clients

"AVN tools such as their Benchmarking and Business Potential software are central to our methodology and our success. They are quick and easy for us to use, and clients really value both the insights they give and the simplicity of the presentation."

Example of Excellence 26
Chris Booth of McKellens Limited

Fundamental change for a 100 year old firm

"AVN tools are at the heart of what we do. They have been central to positioning us as business advisors rather than 'just accountants'. And they have helped us to generate more leads, convert more of those leads into clients and earn higher fees from new and existing clients alike."

Example of Excellence 28
Gloria Murray of Murray Associates

Taking massive action

"A key factor in our success has been the systems, software, tools and support we get from AVN, since they have given us the means and inspiration to make many of these improvements. And they have really allowed us to punch above our weight."

Example of Excellence 36
Ian Main of Stark Main

Two director start-up that has grown to over £800,000 in 5 years

"It would be remiss of me not to also acknowledge the profoundly important role Steve Pipe and his team, have played in helping us to achieve all of this.

From a client perspective their resources, such as the Performance Measurement and Improvement system, which we have put at the heart of what we do for clients, their tax planning software, and their profit improvement tools are incredible differentiators.

Clients love them, with one recently saying to me "This approach is so unusual for your 'breed'. To be analysing and suggesting improvement is so refreshing!" They help us to really impress banks, win more clients, and convince even the most hard-nosed entrepreneurs of the need to pay premium fees. They also help us to give our clients a better and more proactive service, which in turn means that they go on to buy additional services from us.

While, from a firm perspective, much of what we have done has been inspired, informed and enabled by their insights, guidance, support and tools.

I know for a fact that without their help everything would have been so much harder, and some things would not have been possible at all."

Example of Excellence 41
Alan Woods of Woods Squared

Start up sole practitioner with average fees of £8,900 per client

"The tools, software, insights, systems and training we have received as a result of our membership of AVN have been central to our success. Put simply, we wouldn't have been able to achieve anywhere near as much without them.

For example, they provided the Mastery group in Step 1, the One Page Plan system in Step 2, and the client grading system in Step 3. They also created the diagnostic review software, pricing software, tax planning software, sensitivity software and Team Matters software that we use to make our lives so much easier and our service so much better.

But perhaps most importantly of all, they have provided the inspiration, motivation, encouragement and support we really needed to actually make things happen."

The products and services that helped them to become the best

This appendix lists all of the products and services specifically mentioned as useful by the featured practices in their entries in this book.

AVN products and services

1. **Benchmark** – software for benchmarking practices and their clients

2. **Business Builder Forum / BBF** – set of resources containing the systems and content firms need to run a business club for clients and contacts

3. **BoardView** – system for having regular structured meetings with clients

4. **Business Improvement Programme /Business Success Club** – business club run by an experienced business coach on behalf of a firm

5. **Business Potential** – profit improvement sensitivity software

6. **Financial Performance Review** – software for producing five year trend analysis reports

7. **"How to get an extra £2 million"** – seminar using a case study of how a business initially turning over £100,000 got an extra £2 million in cash over a 25 year period by working with a really good accountant

8. **Incorporation Tax Planner** – software for showing clients the tax saving from incorporating – and value pricing the resulting work

9. **One Page Plan** – goal based measurement, target setting, action planning and control system for managing a business using a single A4 sheet of paper

10. **OnTrack** – diagnostic review software for producing Key Improvement Possibilities reports for clients containing proactive recommendations tailored to their specific needs

11. **Penn Report** – tax strategy that, in effect, makes expansion profits free of tax for five or more years after the launch of a major new product, service or division

12. **PMI / "The Numbers"** – A4 folder containing a performance measurement and improvement system for everything that matters in a business

13. **Remuneration Tax Planner** – software for showing clients the lowest tax cost ways of extracting profits from their companies

14. **Simple Stuff That Works** – multi-media profit improvement software

15. **System Builder** – software for systemising an accountancy practice – also contains a library of over a thousand ready-to-use systems, tools and resources to make the task easier

16. **Team Matters** – software for capturing feedback and improvement suggestions from colleagues and team members

17. **Times Up** – pricing software designed to be used live in front of clients – also produces fixed price agreements

For more information on any of the above AVN tools and support visit www.avn.co.uk, phone 0845 2262371 or email info@avn.co.uk

Products and services from other suppliers

1. **2020 membership group** – training and resources for accountants – www.the2020group.com

2. **Academy For Growth** – marketing resources – www.academyforgrowth. co.uk

3. **"Beat the recession"** – book by Nicholas Bate – Published in 2008 by Infinite Ideas and available on www.amazon.co.uk

4. **BNI** – Business networking and referrals club – www.bni.com

5. **Camtasia** – software for making multi media videos out of whatever you put on your computer – www.techsmith.com

6. **DISC** – behavioural profiling system that builds a description of a person's typical behaviours, likely motivations, and approach to life and work – a google search will identify many suppliers

7. **Facebook** – social media and social networking site – www.facebook.com

8. **FAME** – online database of businesses with extensive data analysis functionality – www.bvdinfo.com

9. **IRIS Practice Management** – software for managing a practice – www.iris.co.uk

10. **LinkedIn** – online social networking tool specifically for professionals and others in business – www.linkedin.com

11. **Michael Heppell** – keynote speaker and best selling author – www. michaelheppell.com

12. **Paul Shrimpling** – keynote speaker and adviser to the accountancy profession – www.remarkablepractice.com

13. **Practice DNA** – practice management software developed by one of the firms featured in this book, Hallidays, which they may be willing to make available to like-minded firms who want to move away from timesheets as the source of the key metrics for their business – contact managing partner Nigel Bennett on nigel@hallidays.co.uk

14. **Results Only Work Environment / ROWE** – human resource management strategy described in detail in Daniel Pink's bestselling book "Drive" – available on www.amazon.co.uk

15. **Rypple** – online software for team members to engage, communicate and coach more effectively – www.rypple.com

16. **Strategic Planning Toolkit** – software planning tool for consultants – www.hwli.co.uk

17. **Tax Club** – association for tax professionals chaired by Tim Good – low cost with over 1,400 members – www.mytaxclub.co.uk (Note from editor: for completeness it is also worth mentioning the sister organisation, The Accountants Club, which is chaired by Mark Lloydbottom and has over 750 members – www.myaccountantsclub.co.uk)

18. **Tax Credits Team** – software and resources to help accountants do tax credits compliance and planning work for clients www.taxcreditsteam. co.uk

19. **Traffic Light Feedback system** – online system for getting feedback from clients and customers – www.trafficlightfeedback.co.uk

20. **Twitter** – social networking service – www.twitter.com

21. **Will Kintish** – keynote speaker who specialises in online and offline networking – www.kintish.co.uk

Thanks and acknowledgements

A research project on this scale is only possible because of the efforts, energy and unwavering commitment of an extraordinary group of people.

I would therefore like to thank the entire team at AVN, and especially my brother Michael and my business partner and friend Mark Wickersham, for their encouragement and support over the years in general, and over these last two years in particular.

Of course, I also owe a huge debt of gratitude to my research team: Eleanor Gaffney, Jonathan Pipe, Katie Pipe and Sam Bonser.

I am also extremely grateful to my editor Caroline Swain for doing an excellent job in very little time, and coping so well with my idiosyncrasies, and to David Maister for his invaluable comments on the initial manuscript.

This book could not have been written without the support of my wife Carol. Thank you for giving me the love, energy and space to do the things I am passionate about. I hope I am able to repay you in full.

I would also like to thank Jonathan Holroyd for a lifetime of dedication to the accountancy profession. His passion and enthusiasm have been an inspiration to me and thousands of other accountants. And his unrivalled insights into what makes accountants successful have helped me and many others become better at what we do. I therefore feel very privileged to have him as a colleague and as a friend.

Most importantly of all, I shall be forever indebted to all those firms that shared their stories with me, including those who didn't quite make the final cut. They all did so with extraordinary generosity of spirit, without any form of payment, and in more detail and with more candour than I could have dared to imagine, let alone expect.

In my opinion they have all done the accountancy profession, and the clients it acts for, a profound service.

About the author

Steve Pipe is a Chartered Accountant who is passionate about helping accountants to become more successful by serving their clients better, and is widely regarded as one of the world's leading strategists to the accountancy profession.

His books include *101 ways to make more profits*, *Stress proof your business and your life*, and *Your blueprint for a better tax practice* (with Mark Wickersham FCA). He has also written over 150 training videos for the Accountants' Education Channel and the eight part BBC television series *Easy Money*.

As a keynote speaker, seminar leader and webinar presenter Steve trains thousands of accountants a year. In addition, over the last few years his acclaimed "How to get an extra £2.3 million" seminar has filled venues in every corner of the UK, touching the lives of thousands of business owners.

He is the Founder and Head of Research for AVN, an association of over 200 proactive UK accountancy firms, which was named as one of the 100 most visionary businesses in the UK in the inaugural Vision 100 Index. While his many other awards include being named the "UK Entrepreneur of the Year" by Accountancy Age magazine and the Best Contributor to accountingweb.co.uk.

Steve is married with three children, lives in Leeds surrounded by the glorious Yorkshire countryside, plays tennis and guitar badly, and supports Watford FC and Leeds United football clubs.

Free help from the author

Contact me on steve.pipe@avn.co.uk and I will gladly send you all of the following to help you improve your practice:

- **Free diagnostic tool** – This will help you to evaluate your firm in the light of the content of this book, identify your real strengths and weaknesses, and decide where to focus your efforts

- **Free action planning tool** – Following on from the diagnostic tool, this contains a complete system for formulating and prioritising an action plan that will get you results

- **Free training** – I run many full day seminars and training courses a year for accountants based on the issues in this book. When you contact me I will give you details of at least one such course that you can attend as my guest.

Of course, you are also welcome to tap into my help and support on a paid for basis!

Steve Pipe FCA

steve.pipe@avn.co.uk

0845 2262371

www.avn.co.uk

www.stevepipe.com